Blogging

(3 Books in 1)

Anthony James

Published By: Anthony James

Copyright © All rights reserved

No part of this publication may be copied, reproduced in any format, by any means electronic or otherwise, without prior consent from the copyright owner and publisher of this book.

Table of Contents

Blog Writing:
The Content Creation Blueprint

Introduction 10

Chapter One 13
   Content Planning: Understanding Why You Need to Create Content Consistently? 13

Chapter Two 24
Power-Packed Headline Creation Strategies 24

Chapter Three 34
   Secrets for Curating and Rewriting Great Content 34

Chapter Four: 56
14 Types of Content That Can Sky-Rocket Your Blog Traffic 56

Chapter Five: 70
   10 Content Marketing Tips to Take Your Blog into the Next League 70

Conclusion 77

Blog Writing:

Advanced Strategiesto Monetize Your Blog

Introduction.. 81
Chapter 1: Advanced Strategies to Monetize Your
    Blog...82
Chapter 2: Making Money Through Advertising
    on Your Blog...88
Chapter 3: Monetizing Through Product Creation....94
    Chapter 4: Monetizing Your Blog Through
    Affiliate Marketing...98
    Chapter 5: Monetizing Your Blog Through
    Coaching Services 103
Chapter 6: The Importance of Content Delivery 108
Chapter 7: Monetizing Through Sponsored Posts.... 111
    Chapter 8: Remarketing to Become a Paid
    Blogger 116
Chapter 9: Monetizing Through Email Lists 121
Chapter 10: Monetizing Through Pay Per Click 127
    Chapter 11: Selling Services & Hosting Virtual
    Summits 130
Conclusion 136

Blog Writing:
Traffic Generation Secrets, Hints and Tips

Introduction 140

Part I: Introduction to Traffic Generation 142

Chapter 1: What is Traffic Generation 142

Chapter 2: Make Sure to Get the Right Traffic 145

Part II: Traffic Generation Tips 149

Chapter 3: The Importance of Content When Generating Traffic 149

Chapter 4: Streamline Blog Design to Bring Traffic 153

Chapter 5: Social Media Matters When Driving Traffic 159

Chapter 6: Basic SEO Tips for Traffic Generation 164

Chapter 7: Offer Additional High-Quality Content Outside Your Blog 174

Chapter 8: Comment on Other Blogs and Network with Other Bloggers 178

Chapter 9: Email Marketing 182

Chapter 10: The Power of Guest Posting 188

Chapter 11: Paid Advertising 193

**Part III: How to Keep Your Traffic
Coming Back 196**

Chapter 12: Repurpose Old Content 196

Chapter 13: Engage with Your Audience 200

Conclusion 203

Blog Writing

The Content Creation Blueprint

(How to Master Content Creation to Propel Your Blog On to the Next Level and Make Even More Serious Money Online)

Anthony James

© Copyright 2018 by Anthony James

All rights reserved.

The following eBook is reproduced below with the goal of providing information that is as accurate and reliable as possible. Regardless, purchasing this eBook can be seen as consent to the fact that both the publisher and the author of this book are in no way experts on the topics discussed within and that any recommendations or suggestions that are made herein are for entertainment purposes only. Professionals should be consulted as needed prior to undertaking any of the action endorsed herein.

This declaration is deemed fair and valid by both the American Bar Association and the Committee of Publishers Association and is legally binding throughout the United States.

Furthermore, the transmission, duplication or reproduction of any of the following work, including specific information, will be considered an illegal act irrespective of if it is done electronically or in print. This extends to creating a secondary or tertiary copy of the work or a recorded copy and is only allowed with express written consent from the Publisher. All additional right reserved.

The information in the following pages is broadly considered to be a truthful and accurate account of facts and as such any inattention, use or misuse of the information in question by the reader will render any resulting actions solely under their purview. There are no scenarios in which the publisher or the original author of this work can be in any fashion deemed liable for any hardship or damages that may befall them after undertaking information described herein.

Additionally, the information in the following pages is intended only for informational purposes and should thus be thought of as universal. As befitting its nature, it is presented without assurance regarding its prolonged validity or interim quality. Trademarks that are mentioned are done without written consent and can in no way be considered an endorsement from the trademark holder.

Introduction

Assume you walk into a store to buy a bottle of perfume. The salesperson greets you warmly and goes on to ask you the fragrance you are looking for. He/she chats with you about your typical usage, preferences, and habits. Do you need a more flirty, casual fragrance or a more formal, long-wearing one? Do you keep reusing it often throughout the day or is a one-time application good enough to last throughout the day? The salesperson also informs you about the latest products, how smell affects your mood and other interesting and fascinating details. You strike up a conversation, and before you know, you have bought a ton of stuff from them.

Compare this with walking into a shop and being pitched the most expensive fragrances available without trying to understand what you are looking for or offering you any information (i.e., value) about your purchases. There's no attempt to strike a dialogue or offer value. The person is simply interested in selling rather than helping you buy.

Little wonder then, that you will not buy as much in the second scenario unless you know exactly what you want, and you will be scooting out once you have bought your items without establishing any buyer relationship with the salesperson.

Now think of your blog as the store and your audience as your buyers. Can you simply pitch your business opportunity to internet users without establishing a connection of trust with them? Can you create a loyal community of readers without establishing your authority and credibility?

Hear this loud and clear: people are tired of being spammed and being exposed to a truckload of promotional crap every day. They seek value. Real, solid and relevant value. They are looking for material that is valuable to them and can be quickly applied in their life to solve their most pressing concerns or make things easier for them.

If you are not focusing on a clear content strategy or not sharing real value, you are leaving a ton of money on the table for your competitors. Real, targeted and interested customer leads can be generated only when people are convinced that you can offer them real value.

While spamming social media pages may seem like a quick fix solution to generate some speedy leads, it is a dead end for businesses that will be around for a long time. If you are looking to build a solid, stable and consistent source of long-term income, content is the life blood of your business. The most profitable and leveraged way to get customers to buy from you is to offer them solid value.

Great content helps in building your brand. It also helps in establishing your authority in the given domain. (Who doesn't prefer buying from an expert who knows everything about a particular niche?) A strong content strategy creates sufficient interest in and awareness of your product. Integrating content into the sales process makes it all the more efficient than simply pushing your product on the customer. It makes your brand comes across as likable, relatable, identifiable and human. No one likes to be sold to by bots. Buyers love to buy from real humans with whom they can establish connections. And what better way to establish a dialogue with people than giving them valuable and powerful content that has the potential to impact their lives?

A strong, clear and consistent content strategy helps you build a following of loyal customers who make repeat purchases from you. You do not just make new customers; you also retain the existing ones by offering them sheer value.

Let's dive head first into this fascinating world of content marketing, and begin to master content creation to put your blog on the highway to success.

Chapter One

Content Planning: Understanding Why You Need to Create Content Consistently?

You might be wondering why must you have a clear, coherent and long-term content plan.

Don't misunderstand. Having a content plan or strategy does not mean mapping out every piece of content you will post for the coming year. It simply means that you establish a set of parameters and guidelines for content creation to accomplish specific, higher objectives as you progress.

The goals can be things such as increasing your followers, converting followers into buyers or turning buyers into loyal, repeat customers.

Here are the top reasons why you should have a clear content plan/strategy and consistent content in place if you are serious about turning your blog into a money making machine.

1. Long Term Gains

Think about it. Would you rather invest in one-time scattered promotional or long-term content that requires work once and then can be leveraged multiple times? You create a well-researched, insightful and detailed blog post once and your audience will lap it up for several years to come, without it requiring any additional work from you.

That is the beauty of earning passive income online. You work once and reap its benefits almost forever. Having a blog populated with valuable content gives you the opportunity to earn revenue from it steadily and consistently.

2. Streamlined Efforts

Working on a blog without a clear content plan is like driving to an unknown destination without a map (or Google Maps for millennials). Plans streamline your content and give your blog a sense of direction. Production becomes easier when you have planned ahead about what goes into the blog.

Content can be anything from a holiday season infographic, a timely review of a new product or a detailed, analytical piece created to establish your authority and drive sales during a particular season. Long term content planning gives a clear focus on creating timely content and powerful content ideas to fulfill business goals.

3. Brings Steadiness and Consistency

Have you ever invested in the stock market? You do not always get immediate returns unless you are really lucky and even then that is more likely be an exception than rule.

You cannot build a successful blog simply by creating a couple of viral posts, and hoping they will work wonders for you. A solid content strategy ensures you have a regular and steady flow of content over a period of time, some of which can work brilliantly for you.

Driving traffic to your blog is all about the law of averages at the end of the day. No one really knows what will become a viral sensation that drives thousands of visitors to your blog. You need to have a lot of quality content on your blog if you wish to make money from it because you do not know what posts will work and what will not. A steady flow of content ensures you are not investing all your precious resources into a few posts that you hope will go viral.

For instance, if you have a hundred posts on your blog, even if only 25 to 30 perform exceptionally well, you may well be laughing your way to the bank. It is all a game of numbers so the higher the number of great quality posts you put on your blog, the higher your chances will be of making consistent profits from it.

4. Time Saving

Imagine a scenario where you are managing multiple blogs. Can you really invest time on each of them daily or would you rather plan and keep their content ready in advance to simply post at a convenient time each day? Also, imagine waking up each day and not knowing what to write or post for the day.

Planning your content strategy saves times and allows you to cover days when you may be busier than usual. It is easier to multitask when you have everything ready in advance. You do not waste time trying to figure out what to do next. You invest some time, in the beginning, to put a plan in place and implement it on a weekly or daily basis to fulfill your blogging goals.

5. Boosted Lead Conversions

A well-planned content strategy means making consistent efforts to get your readers to spend greater time on your blog, thus engaging them to boost your conversion rate. Useful content builds trust and sets the stage for people to buy from you. The results may not be immediate, but they can be surprisingly large! Think of it as harvesting a crop.

When you sow the seeds on your farm land, the returns or results are not immediate. You keep watering the seeds, use good quality fertilizers and undertake periodic weeding to reap a rich harvest. The end result? You harvest a flourishing batch of crops after a period of time.

Blogging is really no different. You sow the seeds of great content on your blogging farmland. You water it periodically by updating the content, weed out the spam, and use proven software tools to help you reap rich rewards from loyal, engaged readers who trust you. Credibility, authority, and expertise boost conversions and help you accomplish the desired results. The results may not be instant, but over a period of time you could end up reaping rich rewards from your consistent efforts.

Remember the salesperson example at the beginning of the book? The salesperson who builds a rapport with his/her customer has higher chances of making the sale over someone who does not care to build a rapport.

Readers are likelier to buy from you when you help them buy and don't merely try to sell.

6. Higher Search Engine Rank

Don't try to kid yourself by saying you are not writing for Google or you do not care about search engines. The fact is, however strong your promotion/marketing/advertising strategy is, everyone can do with a little organic promotion boost. Even though search engines have highly complicated algorithms that are tough to crack, it is fairly safe to say that content is a vital component of it.

Using the right keywords, creating detailed and well-researched content relevant to those keywords, and using multiple presentation formats (videos, photographs, infographics) boost your chances of ranking high on search engines.

Well-optimized blogs that have the right keywords and backlinks are favorably viewed by the big G and other search engines. It is no secret that Google loves long, detailed, visual-rich posts that pack in plenty of informational value for the reader.

They want to improve their user experience and hence rank posts that offer users detailed and relevant information in an easily digestible format.

Content planning equips you with the ability to create a steady flow of content for boosting your SEO efforts. The more content you create, the higher your chances will be of being found on search engines by your target market.

7. Higher Traffic

More keywords and focused blog posts mean reaching a higher number of interested readers, who will be keen to know more about your products or services. Imagine having a single post that's performing/ranking well on search engines. You will draw readers who are interested in reading that particular post.

Now, imagine a few hundred posts performing well on search engines. Can you image your organic reach and the number of people you will be drawing to your blog? Also, more posts mean greater sharing on social media, which can be a goldmine for targeted customers. If you have multiple thoughtfully written and interesting posts going viral, your blog will draw higher traffic.

People invariably share content that makes them look smart and well-informed among their social circle. If you take the trouble to put together a content plan about creating awesome content you are literally saying to people, "come share this great piece of content with your friends to show them how well-read and smart you are." This leads to more sharing, a greater buzz about your blog, and eventually higher traffic. Not bad for a little streamlined planning!

8. Creates a Desirable Brand

A clear, creative and strong content strategy helps create awareness about your brand. It helps your audience identify with the brand and connect with them at a subconscious level to make your brand more desirable. It is easier to get people to buy from you when they can connect with your brand values.

Content creation helps you create a more identifiable and likable brand that people can relate to. Say for instance you have a blog dedicated to helping people who are going through a painful marriage or relationship. You make money by promoting other people's eBooks (affiliate marketing) on saving marriages or preparing for a divorce.

When you create posts that resonate with people (how to help your children cope with a separation or how to help children heal after breaking away from an abusive relationship) and offer them solutions, they can relate to your brand.

When people identify and relate to your brand, it is easier for them to forge connections and buy from you. A strong content strategy demonstrates that you know enough about a subject to make expert, life-improving recommendations to them. Great content invariably creates a desirable and irresistible brand that people love to follow.

Engaged followers/readers make for more willing buyers. They are more open to recommendations and solutions originating from an authoritative source. In an era where businesses mushroom by the hour, great content prevents people from forgetting your brand. Engaged users are some of the best evangelists for your brand. They help to endorse your brand without a need for you to aggressively promote it in coming years.

When people read anything on your blog, they are unknowingly forming an impression about your brand values. If they come across content that is informative, insightful and enlightening, they are likely to think positively about your brand. If they see your content consistently shared on social media, your brand appears more established and trustworthy in the industry.

9. Establishes Expertise

Consistently writing high-quality posts boosts the perceived authority, expertise and credibility of your blog. When other blogs link to your well-written posts, your blog domain authority increases. It acts as a sort of validation for your expertise among your target audience.

Higher domain authority again translates into boosted search engine rankings, which makes your blog content even more visible. Great quality content created through smart content planning strategies increases your blog's organic visibility.

Audience recognition and connections are an important strategy for any business, and blogging is no exception. If you use individuals to create and share content, people could develop a closer association or more intimate relationship with them, and eventually your brand. You will become their go-to place for any information related to the topic, thus strengthening their loyalty.

Basics of Content Planning

1. Set content goals. What is the main objective of your content strategy? Who are the end users of the content? What do you want them to gain from the content? What should be covered in the content? The objectives should be clearly communicated to your team of writers and

designers so the content and design are consistent.

2. Create Timelines. Sticking to a schedule is extremely important when it comes to content creation. Your chances of profiting from your posts increase when you post consistently on schedule. It can be a blog post a day, or two to three posts spread throughout the week. However you do it, posting regularly is a must if you want to build a steady income from it.

3. Document a strategy. Create a sheet where everyone can reference the team's content creation strategy to eliminate miscommunication. Put together an editorial calendar that lists the blog topic, the name of the author and the date the post is scheduled to be published.

4. Ensure deadlines are met. Equip your team of writers or designers with the available resources to turn around quick and high-quality work that is on schedule. Defaulting on deadlines means your content does not go up at the scheduled, which can result in a loss of engagement and revenue.

Chapter Two

Power-Packed Headline Creation Strategies

Now that we know why creating content consistently is so important, and the basics of content planning, it's time to notch up the learning a bit. Let's learn more about creating awesome, mind-blowing content that your readers just cannot get enough of. What is it that distinguishes average content from fabulous pieces that are shared all over the internet? Here are some expert content creation tips.

Secret Formula for Crafting Sticky Blog Headlines

(There I had your attention, didn't I?)

"On the average, five times as many people read the headline as read the body copy. When you have written your headline, you have spent eighty cents out of your dollar."
—David Ogilvy

The headline is really the backbone of your content. Of course, you cannot simply create a brilliant headline to peddle lousy content. However, an attention-grabbing, eye-catching and interesting headline can give huge momentum to your content piece.

The trouble most bloggers or writers have is that they spend hours writing the perfect blog copy and devote little time to the headline. This means the post fails to grab their reader's attention. And unfortunately, this means the perfectly written blog copy does not get read.

Did you know that nearly 8 out of 10 people read just a headline, while only 2 out of 10 take time to read the entire post? A great headline can increase the number of visitors on your blog.

It will boost the chances of your content being read and shared by readers.

So what are some of the best tips for writing sticky headlines?

1. **Appeal to people's most primal emotions**

Emotions such as fear, joy, unhappiness, humor, etc. Make your headlines a mix of emotion and logic. Reinforce a problem and pitch your post as a solution for that problem.

Headlines should first grab people's attention by appealing to a strong emotion, and then compel them to read it by offering a solution or strong value proposition. For instance:

Struggling to Come Up with the Perfect Blog Headline? Here Are Some Fool-Proof Tips!

Worried About Your Student Loans? Here's Our Secret Formula for Leading a Debt Free Life!

Begin with a rough, working title. You most likely will not have your 'wow' headline dawn upon you in a Eureka moment (though as you practice, this will happen more often).

A working title gives a clear angle to a broad topic. It gives a specific guideline tone to the post while making it more targeted. For instance, raising intelligent kids can be a fairly broad topic, which people may have seen on a hundred other blogs about parenting.

However, you can make it super specific by using a headline such as "10 Foods That Can Strengthen Your Child's Memory" or "Quick Mind Exercises to Sharpen Your Kid's Brain." Contrast these headlines with "How to Raise Intelligent Kids?" The first headlines are more specific and attention grabbing. They are clear about what readers can expect in the post.

The broad headline does not pique your curiosity because it seems vague and does not tell you precisely what aspect of raising intelligent children is being covered in the post.

Did you know that in an attention starved world where people are constantly bombarded with information, they decide whether they want to spend time reading or not reading something within seconds?

Start with a specific working title (keep it narrow), and keep working on it as you create your post copy. Once you have a headline to guide your post, you can keep improving it until you are ready to publish.

2. Stay Factual and Accurate.

Set the right expectations while writing headlines for your blogs. A headline like, "20 Companies Who Are Slaying It with Twitter So Freaking Amazingly They Do Not Use Other Advertising Channels" is slightly pretentious and quite over the top. Do not make bombastic, exaggerated claims for some quick page views.

This is nothing but a form of click bait, where you create misleading, false or inaccurate headlines just to get people to click on a link. It can end up hurting the credibility and authenticity of your blog heavily. If you are in it for the long haul, avoid inaccurate headlines like the plague.

3. Use the power of numbers.

If you head to your nearest grocery store and scan through a magazine or tabloid headlines, you will notice how they effectively use numbers to grab the reader's attention. Strange as it may seem, obscure numbers are believed to grab the reader's attention. So now you know, why those "37 Perfect Destinations for A Summer Wedding" or "11 Easy and Healthy Drinks to Beat Your Summer Blues" are so popular.

4. Tap into people's hot buttons by using "trigger" words.

There is always a more effective and impactful way to convey an idea. Include actionable verbs and interesting adjectives that cause people to read the post.

So, you can have a headline like, "Top 10 Things to Do When You Are Feeling Depressed."

Or you can convey the same idea with, "10 Incredible Ways to Beat Depression." We just re-packaged the headline into something more enticing and attractive by including an actionable verb and compelling adjective.

Headlines are all about saying a lot with very few words. Try to communicate the essence of your post while still using as few words as possible to retain its impact.

Use words such as effortless, genuine, honest, free, fun, essential, strange, incredible, absolute, delighted, proven, secrets, tricks, ideas and other similar terms to gain people's attention and trust.

5. Make it Bold.

Promise your reader something insanely valuable and fulfill that promise. It can be anything such as learning new skills, persuading the reader to do something they have never done before or unlocking a mystery. Offer the reader a bold and clear value proposition.

What you are doing is daring the reader to read the post. Be bold without overpromising or sounding preposterous. Be seductive (not in the literal sense, of course) and dangerous. And then deliver.

6. Make it sexy aye!

Have some fun and make your title eye popping and sexy. Add a dash of zing to it by understanding your buyer's primary persona. Use words and phrases that resonate with the reader.

Playing with alliteration is a good idea for drafting sexy sounding headlines. Phrases like

"Secret Strategies" and "Fool-Proof Formula" have a subtle yet powerful impact.

Strong language also makes for sexy headlines, even if you use negative language to create a bit of a stir, such as "Things -------- Hate." However, make sure you are using the negative technique in moderation. If you try to make everything bold instead of keeping a few things bold, the gravity of the boldness is lost.

7. Keep your headlines short.

There is no standard size for a headline of course, but it should be succinct and crisp enough to keep your reader hooked. Do not make it long winded and verbose. Keep it brief, pithy and interesting. If you make your blog title more than 70 characters, it will be slashed by search engines, thus weakening its impact.

If you are trying to optimize your blog title for social media, headlines should ideally stay between 8-14 words.

8. Follow a simple yet highly effective formula.

Numerical (or a powerful trigger word) + adjective + main/secondary keyword + solution/promise.

For instance, if you are writing about bathing puppies, you could say *18 Incredible Ways to Bathe a Puppy Outdoors.*

Think about writing a headline making a bold promise applying this formula. For instance, to sell your old furniture in a day, the headline could be *How You Can Easily Sell Your Old Furniture in Less Than 24 Hours.* People really do not want to invest precious time reading something boring. They want action-packed and exciting content. These are the headlines that get your content read, and eventually, it will boost conversions.

Make reading the blog post worth people's time by creating headlines that not only grab their attention but also describe your post in an accurate, honest and enticing manner. Make it a proposition they cannot refuse, and an action they will not regret.

Here are some brilliant headline formulas

1. Do You Want To -------- Like Your Friends?

This is a classic social proof headline that tells the reader that many others are doing what is advertised or mentioned in the blog. It instills a fear of not wanting to be left behind. The reader should feel like they will miss something if they do not read the content or click on the link.

2. Here is One Neat Technique That is Really Helping People --------
3. Little Known Strategies For ---------
4. Here's a Quick and Effective Way to -------
5. Warning! You May Be ------- (something unflattering)
6. 10 Proven Ways to (accomplishing a desired goal)
7. What You Should Know About --------- (something that impacts their life)
8. Are You Still Stuck with Eating Dairy? (Pose provocative questions that get your readers thinking).
9. 25 Hacks to (accomplishing the desired result). Easy yet effective, solution offering headline. It gets people looking for quick solutions hooked.
10. Now You Can Really Have ------------ (something desirable)
11. 15 Experts Share their Number One Child Nutrition Tip (the round-up headline when you featuring experts/influencers in your niche to create a round-up for your blog)
12. How Eating Fruits and Vegetables Can Make You Fat (the unexpected pattern breaking headline. You can also use a reminder headline like Your Weight Doesn't Really Reveal Your Health.

Anything unexpected that challenges commonly accepted notions have a novelty factor attached to it, which makes people take notice. However, ensure that the headline is in sync with your content. If your headline says that eating vegetables can make you fat then mention in what way vegetables can make you fat. Do not create false headlines just to grab the reader's attention.

9. Use Topic generator sites and tools.

This one is a little known tip yet is my favorite for generating lots of cool blog post ideas and headlines.

Use a site like SEOPressor to come up with a bunch of search engine optimized (SEO) friendly and engaging headlines. You enter a keyword. Let's say acne, then go on to describe the keyword (is it is generic term or brand/product name, etc).

The results will return several attractive blog topics and headlines such as "5 Secrets About Acne Which Haven't Been Revealed in the Last 50 Years" or "You Will Never Believe These Bizarre Truths About Acne." HubSpot's blog topic generator is also worth using. Look at these sites for inspiration.

Chapter Three

Secrets for Curating and Rewriting Great Content

We know by know what a difference wow content and attention grabbing headlines can make when it comes to developing a seriously profitable blog. However, how do you constantly come up with power-packed content that interests and impact readers?

Fret not, I have your back there. I am spilling all the beans about digging out super powered content that has the potential to make your blog massively successful.

Content Curation

While content creation is about creating a piece of content (blog post, video, image or more) from scratch, curation is about gathering already existing content such as blog posts, social media updates or eBooks that are relevant to your niche, and sharing them with your readers/followers.

Several surveys have revealed that the number one challenge for blog owners or content marketers is to come up with sufficient quality content to build a more engaged social media audience and populate their blogs with top notch content.

Though it has its share of limitations, content curation has the following benefits:

- It helps build relationships with other bloggers and influencers. Content curation is like a brilliant synergy where everyone benefits from giving each other a larger audience. It helps build some amazing online partnerships with industry influencers.
According to a Crowdtap study, 44% of industry experts work with other brands since it offers them a relevant opportunity for their audience, too.
- Content Curation saves time. If you are operating multiple blogs and social media channels, and do not have the time to populate each of them with stellar content on a daily basis, content curation is like manna from heaven for your blog.
- Admit it. You cannot be a pro at everything. Content curation helps you fill the gaps that you may have left as a creator. Sourcing content from diverse, reputable channels gives you the advantage of bringing more variety to your content.

Having said that, ensure that if you use content from other sources, link attribution is given to the writer and blog page. Seek proper permissions before using someone else's content. Ensure that the terms are clear before posting, so there's no confusion or legal hassles later.

Have you heard about Upworthy? Yes, the same viral site that posts interesting content with catchy, clickbait style headlines.

When they launched, they became a roaring success only by repackaging and curating a majority of their content from other sources and posting it using sexy and shocking headlines. They eventually transitioned into content creation, but a lot of the early success was their ability to repackage promising content from varied sources and presenting it in a more stunning, attention-grabbing style.

4 Ways for Finding Great Content in Your Niche

1. Go to a BuzzSumo. Enter your topic or domain in the search option, and click go. You will be presented with the most popular content related to your topic, including statistics such as numbers of social media shares and pages that link back to it.

2. Google Trends is another great place for digging out great content based on organic searches. So, if you want to have a nice combination of content that is popular on both social media and search engines, include Google Trends into your content curation strategy. You will see an entire list of trending stories for the last 24 hours. Enter a specific topic if you want to gauge the changing popularity of a topic and the interest it generates among readers of varied geographic regions.

3. A lot of viral sites pick up their content from aggregators such as Reddit. It is indeed the "Front Page of the Internet" as it describes itself. There's a goldmine of hidden content in subreddits on virtually any topic under the sun.

   Unlike other content aggregation channels, Reddit's content is ranked by freshness and popularity score, which makes it an ideal platform for digging out trending content, especially about lesser known niches.

   On signing up, a user automatically has access to a a large amount of content. You have to manually unsubscribe from subreddits that aren't of any interest to you. There's plenty of opportunity to get your hands on little known, detailed, multiperspective and information-rich content.

4. Use the power of question and answer sites. Quora is another great place for finding informative and detailed content presented as answers to a query by most experts in their fields. So you may have skin experts offering the best home remedies for black heads or a practicing Stoic sharing his insightful beliefs about the philosophy of Stoicism.

There are other question and answer sites such as Wiki Answers, How Stuff Works and Yahoo Answers, where you can unearth a lot of interesting stuff related to your niche.

5 Stellar Tips Used by Professionals for Rewriting Existing Content

Rewriting has gained a sort of notoriety on the online content world owing to the misconceptions people hold about it. It is not simply altering a few words or inserting a few synonymous to make it appear original.

Rewriting content is about repackaging existing content to lend it a fresh appeal, while still retaining the essence of the original.

If you already have a large bank of blog posts or original content, it is easy to repurpose it into newer and fresher pieces of content instead of starting from scratch and hitting a roadblock. Cut your time by using these valuable strategies for repurposing existing pieces into stellar content.

1. Transform lists into standalone content pieces. If you have several list-based posts such as "7 crackling smart investment options" and other similar posts, you can very well convert it into individual blog posts. Each investment option can be turned into a separate blog post by listing its features, merits, and demerits. Fleshing out each point also gives your readers more detailed and insightful information.

It gives you an opportunity to build on or expand existing ideas by conducting research. Repacking lists into individual articles also establishes your expertise in a specific subject. Add a few case studies or examples to make the posts more comprehensive and interesting to read.

2. Combine multiple posts into a summary post. You may have written multiple blog posts about child psychology or about improving learning and development among children. Use key point from each blog to create a summary blog post like "Top Tips for Improving Your Child's Learning Abilities" or "5 Important Things Parents Must Know About Development Learning." It is actually just the opposite of the first tip.

3. Revamp old posts for a brand new audience. You may have written something keeping in mind a specific audience. For instance, operational challenges faced by nonprofit organizations. You may want to cater to another type of audience; for instance, small business owners. While the general framework will remain similar, you will

have to tweak a few points to suit profit organizations. This will help you target different sets of audience in a more focused manner with almost similar content.

4. Update existing posts with latest information. In today's fast paced world, things change at the blink of an eyelid. There are forever new developments and updates, especially in the world of internet marketing and technology. The blog post you drafted a couple of years ago may be relevant, but there may be newer trends and developments that you readers may want to know.

For instance, if you wrote a post about best SEO practices for bloggers in 2015, you may want to update it by including newer SEO dynamics and trends that held relevance over the past year. Make it a practice to review old blog posts periodically to gauge if they can be updated with fresh statistics, newer examples/case studies or important recent developments. Google and other search engines love fresh, updated and time-relevant content.

5. Focus on ideas, not words. Even the most seasoned writers and bloggers fall into the trap of copying words above ideas. Do not restructure the content sentence by sentence or even paragraph by paragraph just because you are rewriting an existing piece of content. Instead of focusing on expressions and composition of the original writer, try and concentrate on ideas. Rewriting is not about shuffling a few words and sentences. The objective is to understand what exactly is being conveyed, and then communicate it in your own, distinct style.

6. Add fresh, new ideas. Yes, we can all have our Eureka moments while writing, where we think of something fresh and exciting that hasn't been covered by the original writer or our original post. Utilize this moment of epiphany to the fullest, and include these new insights into your post. You may want to include an interesting piece of research or share an example or add your own unique perspective on the matter.

   No rule says one cannot include a fresh element to rewritten content. Do not be afraid to reinvent and improve the post with newer insights. It will only help in making the article appear fresher and more distinct from the original.

7. Re-writing headlines. Alerting the headline to give your post a new angle is the easiest way to begin the rewriting process. Find something that is still relevant to your post but lends it a slightly diverse perspective or angle. You may also want to include a different keyword or optimize the post for Google or social media channels.

8. Make the introductory paragraph unique. The opening paragraph is your chance to grab the interest of your competitor or send them running to competitors. Make it an enticing proposition by including something of value that does not feature in the original article. It can be anything from a statistic to a new piece of research to an attention-grabbing pro tip. Give readers a strong reason to read further even if they have read the original post. Avoid fluff in the opening paragraph (or anywhere in the post).

Another neat tip is to reinvent the layout of your post by including different headings and subheadings. You may want to expand the article by breaking it into sub headings if there aren't any in the original. It will also make your piece more scan-able and readable.

Finding Jaw Dropping Beautiful Images

Images are an important component of your blog profit strategy. They complement your written words to create a more wholesome experience for the reader. All top blogs use attention grabbing images to communicate their message compellingly. Using the right images also boost your search engine optimization efforts.

So how to do you find images that make your blog posts look amazing? Here are some expert tips to find the perfect images for your post.

Take Pictures Yourself

This really saves you the trouble of finding the perfect and most relevant images for your blog. There are no hassles about seeking permissions, paying for high-quality stock photos or digging into the creative commons public domain.

If you are writing a post and have a fair idea about how to represent it best visually, use you a camera or your smartphone to take high-quality pictures. Ensure they are well-lit to make them appear high-resolution images. Go outdoors and take pictures in bright light to make them look more flattering.

Paid Royalty-Free Stock Images

If you have a higher budget, you can buy royalty free images from iStockPhoto or Shutterstock. They have a huge assortment of images for virtually any conceivable topic under the sun.

Bloggers/publishers have the option of paying a one-time fee for using an image several times for various purposes (without any fixed time limit for using it) or sign up for a monthly/yearly subscription that allows you to download a fixed number of images per month/year.

These photographs are high vector images that make your site look professional, and save you from getting into any copyright trouble later.

Free Photo Resources

There are many sites such as Pixabay, Pexels, Unsplash and more where you can get access to a whole bunch of high-quality and on-topic images. Simply enter a few keywords related to the picture in the search option and pick the ones that fit well with your post. Pixabay has a fairly good collection of images, which can be used even for commercial purposes without attribution.

Just ensure that you do not use the sponsored images that show at the top of your search since these are the pay to use images. It is fairly easy to tell because the sponsored images have a distinct watermark.

Ensure you read the terms of every picture you are using very carefully to avoid getting into copyright issues trouble. Some pictures may require an attribution (credit to the owner), some may not.

Even though the prospect of using free images seems lucrative, things change pretty rapidly in the online business world. You never know when the original owner of the image may change its terms of use.

You may not have a large budget in the initial stages of your blog, which makes these free resources a good place, to begin with. Once you start raking in some profits, it is a good idea to invest in royalty-free paid stock images.

Others Blogs and Pages

You cannot simply get images from other people's blogs and pages by performing a simple Google image search. It could lead to serious copyright violations and legal trouble.

If you really like a particular image that's on another blog, begin by complimenting the owner/photo and seek their permission clearly for using the photo. Always seek permission before posting the image and proceed only when you have documented permission stating their consent for using their original work on your blog.

Give them proper credit by mentioning them as the source and linking back to their page or website below the image.

Creative Commons License (CC)

Images under the Creative Commons license are in public domain, which means you are free to use, reuse and distribute them. Depending on individual Creative Commons (CC) licenses, users can use images for commercial purposes or create derivatives of the image.

There are several CC licenses, which means you have to carefully go through the license of each image to know what is permissible under the specific license. To be on the safer side, always attribute all images under the Creative Commons license to their rightful owner.

Wikimedia Commons and Flickr are some great sources for finding CC licensed images. Again while using images from these sources check all licenses by clicking on the individual terms of use/some rights reserved link. You will learn the terms of use of that particular photo such as, whether it can be shared, adapted and used commercially. Also, it will be mentioned if an attribution link to the owner of the image is required.

Here's a quick breakdown of various Creative Commons Licenses

Attribution: This means that the user is required to attribute the image to its original owner in the specified manner. You also have to be mindful of the fact that the image should not be used in a manner which implies that the owner of the image endorses your page/brand or you in any way.

Share-Alike: This clause means the image should not be held under different or restrictive terms than those laid down by the original creator.

Non Commercial: The image should only be utilized for non-commercial purposes.

No Derivative Works: The image is to be used only as it is without altering it or creating derivatives of it.

9 Kick-Ass Resources to Enhance Your Content Writing from Good to Wow

Of course, you have great content and the best formats to present it. However, the tools listed below can expedite the process or make it even more effective. Here are five resources that should be in the tool box of every content creator or marketer.

1. Grammarly

This is really your must have tool when it comes to writing grammatically correct and smooth flowing blogs. The software helps scan your text for any grammatical, punctuation and spelling errors really fast, thus making it appear professional. As a resource, it gives more direction and clarity to your writing. It helps optimize your post and makes it easier to read.

2. Hemingway

Hemingway is a virtual editing tool that is hugely popular among content writers, with good reason. It is a user-friendly text editing software, which highlights complex sentences and offers suggestions for eliminating unwanted adverbs. It also converts drab reading passive sentences into a more actionable active voice.

There is a tracker, which shows you the final count of words, characters, and paragraphs. You can fine-tune the text structure to make it more appealing and readable. Once you are finish making changes, the file can be exported in an .html format.

3. Ideaflip

As a content creator, learn to develop ideas rather than working on the first one that strikes you. Brainstorming is integral to the process of creating wow-worthy content, and Ideaflip helps you do that.

Instead of writing everything on a piece of paper, use Ideaflip. It offers a highly visual, dynamic and interactive platform for developing ideas.

4. Power Thesaurus

Power Thesaurus is a crowdsourced app that does not have any ads (yay!). It is a hit with writers for its elegant interface and streamlined search options. The app is always updated with the newest linguistic trends, which makes it a must-have ammo in your writer warfare kit.

5. Ahrefs

Ahrefs is several SEO resources that can push your blog content into the next league by ranking higher on search engines. Some tools help you keep a close eye on your competitors' SEO tactics and enhance your own content.

6. Canva

We have discussed the power of using compelling visuals in drawing people to your blog. Canva helps you accomplish that goal, with its aesthetically pleasant layouts and high utility value. Use it when you want to add some sparkle to your visual content. It allows graphically challenged folks to create professional and stunning looking visual presentations, infographics and social media cover images. They have a wide assortment of templates that can be adapted for any niche.

7. StackEdit

StackEdit is a handy tool for converting text files into .html or exporting them from Google Docs or Word without altering the formatting. It is an inbuilt browser mark-down that has a ton of great features such as shortcuts that make your writing more unique, has a variety of themes and several layouts. Also, the spell checker is compatible with several languages. The best part? StackEdit can be synced with a variety of tools such as WordPress and Dropbox. It is also available for offline use.

9. Yoast WordPress Plugin

Even though you do not have to stuff your posts with a bunch of keywords, you still have to make your posts more searchable for readers. What's the point of writing phenomenal blog posts when your readers are not able to find them?

Yoast lets you know how optimized your content is regarding a specific keyword and content analysis. It offers tons of helpful suggestions about how to optimize your post to please search engines and readers. It also includes a handy site map feature, which boosts your search engine page indexing efforts.

Content Scheduling

A well-organized and comprehensive content schedule allows you to stay on track with your editorial goals. It helps you save time, and take on multiple tasks, while still running your blog on auto-pilot. Here are some power-packed content scheduling tips.

1. Have a clear brand/blog persona and start by brainstorming content that matches your persona. The content should address your target audience's most pressing issues. Aspire to be a trusted and

respected source of information related to the industry.

2. Plenty of marketers test their content on social media before creating full-fledged blog posts about the same. The experimental post can be thought-provoking, fresh, engaging, humorous and exclusive. Gauge if your content has the potential to be popular on social media.

3. Create a content calendar for 1 to 3 months in advance, and keep adding to it. Bigger events such as Q&A's, interviews, eBooks, product releases, conferences, podcasts, live videos can be announced once a date is locked.

4. Social media posts are best scheduled in advance unless you want to post about recent developments.

5. As a good practice, create 3-4 long blog posts a week, a couple of SlideShare presentations, syndication on sites such Tumblr, 4-5 daily comments from influencers around the web, an infographic every two weeks and a monthly eBook.

6. Google Calendar is a great resource for planning and scheduling content.
7. Keep a close eye on trends too. You may be the most fastidious planner, but you can never completely rely on scheduled content. Keep a close eye on latest trends for cashing in on latest stories. Monitor your content analytics closely. Your content calendar will keep evolving according to your readers' response.

If it is not working for you, try different types of content. Look around at what competitors are doing in a dynamic and ever-changing world of content marketing.

How to Schedule Posts on WordPress

For publishing posts to your audience's time zone, go to the WordPress dashboard and head to settings. Tap on the General Menu option. Select the appropriate time zone and click "Save Changes."

There is a "Publish meta box" on the right-hand corner of the "Edit" option adjacent to the Publish button. Set the date and time the date you wish to publish your post.

Schedule you blog post at the given date and time. Tap on the "Schedule" button.

For rescheduling posts, select "Edit" adjacent to the right-hand side of the Schedule tab. Set the new date and time for publishing the post and update it.

The same process can be used for re-publishing posts that were previously published at a given date and time. You can also create a new post and make it appear as if it was published earlier by following the same process. There are lots WordPress plugins for scheduling posts, too.

Chapter Four:

14 Types of Content That Can Sky-Rocket Your Blog Traffic

There's no short cut to success. If you want to build a profitable blog, you have got to put in a lot of stellar content out there for your audience. Not just that, you have to diversify your content strategy to use different types of content formats that work. There are plenty of fresh and interesting ways to present your content and grow the blog. Don't know how?

Here's a list of different types of content that are proven to draw a large audience, increase engagement, boost SEO and help you build a solid brand.

1. How-to Posts

Everyone loves step-by-step how-to tutorials which make the process of learning something new or solving a problem fairly simple. Any solution showing a how-to post or video is a golden opportunity for attracting a targeted audience. If laid out in an easy-to-understand, step-by-step and detailed manner, these posts/videos perform extremely well and go viral really quick.

Pro Tip: Make it a long and detailed post, almost like a short report or book. It is great if you can include images or screenshots describing each step.

2. Latest News

You will not believe the number of pages that make money on the internet purely on shock value. Of course, unless your blog is an all-news blog, you can also use breaking news related to your industry in combination with other pieces of information.

The biggest advantage of breaking and latest news is that you do not have to create it from scratch. You just have to put together the most important bits of information and rewrite it. Lots of blog owners curate news pieces from other sources and link back to them.

People love to follow interesting or important pieces of information related to their industry or area of interest. It goes a long way in establishing your blog's credibility and authority, which is important if you want to get people to buy from you.

The way to get it right is by opting for quality over quantity. Do not populate your viral fed or blog with too many click-bait style breaking news pieces. Position yourself as an idea influencer in your industry. Offer only high value, useful and insightful content. You can either publish a piece of breaking news daily or create weekly/monthly news updates.

3. Infographics

Infographics are hugely popular, especially when it comes to social sharing. People love to share content that is presented in a comprehensive, yet condensed, format.

Human beings are wired to be attracted to anything that's presented in an easy-to-understand, visual format. We dig interactivity, research, and stats that are packaged in a more digestible form.

Creating appealing and share-worthy infographics is time-consuming. You can do it yourself using an app like Canva or Photoshop if you are more graphically inclined or you can hire someone from elance, Guru or oDesk to do it for you. Visual.ly is also a good place for getting started with infographics.

If you do not want to make your infographics from scratch, share existing ones. There are lots of handy infographics available to be embedded through a simple Google search. Just ensure you have the permission to use it, and credit it to the right source.

4. Lists

Again, it is no secret that people love lists, which explains the barrage of "10 best things to do" and "30 best places to head to" etc. on your social feed. Readers love content that is presented to them in a systematic, digestible and structured manner.

Can you really resist clicking on list-based headlines that sound interesting and informative? This is the classic go to post for any content creator or marketer.

There's a neat little trick to get these posts right. Start by introducing a problem. List possible solutions for the problem, and offer a strong, actionable conclusion that nudges the reader to act upon these solutions.

Provide value to the reader by making these list posts as detailed and comprehensive as possible. Most Important – be sure to give these posts attention-grabbing and nonmisleading headlines. Your "10 Good Content Formats" (even if exceptionally well-written) may not grab as many views as "10 Outrageously Successful Content Formats That You Aren't Using Yet." If you need people to be all ears to your message, convey it with a punch.

Pro Tip: do not just list all the points to read like a grocery list. Take the time to discuss each point, offer your own insights, present numbers and justify the item's inclusion in the list. For instance, if you are telling people Greece is one of the best places for destination weddings in 2017, tell them why too (number of tourist, great weather, visitor friendly conditions, easy laws, etc.). Always focus on offering a strong value proposition to your audience.

5. Round-Ups

Expert round-ups may seem easy because you are not creating the content yourself. However, it may take time and effort to put it all together.

Round-ups are nothing but posts where several experts in your subject share their number one tip or answer a focused question related to topic. For instance, if you are running a blog in the internet marketing domain, you may pose questions such as "What is your number one tip for growing social media followers or generating traffic for your blog?"

Round ups work because they are beneficial for everyone involved. Your readers get access to a whole list of expert tips. The influencers get to reinforce their expert status by sharing your post among their followers and readers. You get plenty of shares from different experts (imagine 20 different experts all sharing your posts among their followers to demonstrate that they have been featured as experts yet again).

However, it is not easy to put together a round-up. You need to approach influencers and get them to agree to be featured in the round-up. However, if you can pull off a few fantastic round-ups, you may manage to draw a swarm of blog traffic.

Some good tools for finding influencers in your niche are BuzzSumo, Traackr, Linkdex and more. You can also search on social media using popular hashtags or keywords related to your niche.

6. PowerPoint Presentations and Slides

This is a highly proven format that seldom goes wrong. It makes for a visual and interactive way to get across information to a focused audience. Slideshare is a great platform for sharing information in a slide show format.

Keep it a mix of information and entertainment. Do not make the readers feel like they are being held hostage in a boring meeting or the boardroom. Even the most serious topic can do with a dash of humor. This is a simple yet highly effective way to put across a ton of information in a quick, understandable format.

7. Case Studies

Case studies are a perfect way to flaunt your expertise in the industry. The ideal way is to take up something that you have worked on yourself. If you can present to your readers how a particular approach helped others meet their goals, etc., you will automatically appear more authoritative and credible to them. If you are selling a product or service on your blog, it is a good idea to include a case study about the value it offered someone. You are doing nothing but validating your product or reinforcing its merit.

A great case study is similar to a how to post, only more focused, insightful and detailed. Sum it up with the lessons readers can take back from it along with a powerful conclusion that gets them thinking. End with a strong call to action.

Pro tip: Do not simply rattle away facts and figures to appear intelligent. Weave the fact and figures into a story to make the case study more relatable and identifiable. Adding a human touch to it makes it more engaging than a clinical approach of merely rattling off facts.

8. Reviews

These are your manna from heaven where blog profits are concerned. Review-based posts are great for affiliate marketers promoting the products and services of others.

Richly written, pictorial and detailed reviews, which are presented in an easy to follow format are hugely lucrative.

Ensure the reviews are broken up into short paragraphs. Include lots of bullet points (pros and cons of a product or service), tables and visuals. Tables can be used to demonstrate what the product or service offers in comparison to similar products or services.

The ideal structure is beginning with an introduction, sharing your experience with the product (merits and demerits), and a conclusion (stating whether you would recommend the product to your readers). Summarize the key points of the review to facilitate quick reading for those who do not have much time at their disposal.

Finally, include a powerful call to action.

9. Guides, eBooks or Short Reports

If you think there is a huge need for detailed and lengthy information related to a particular area of your niche, go ahead and create a detailed guide or short report for it. These are more extensive in content and visuals than blog posts. You can offer your readers to download it in PDF format. What's more?

This can be a huge bait for getting interested readers to sign up for your email list. Enlist the assistance of a graphic designer to help you put together the layout and cover for the guide or report.

If you want to make the value proposition even more, create an entire eBook related to the topic. You will get ideas for the book simply by keeping your ears close to what your readers are saying. For instance, if you own a travel blog and keep posting about your global adventures, readers may ask you about how you manage to travel to so many destinations or your favorite tips for traveling cheap. This is a great opportunity to dive head on into creating an eBook about budget travel tips. You get the drift? Identify an area where people are desperately looking for information within your niche. It does not have to be a 200 page document. You can create a short eBooks with an eye-catching cover and gripping, valuable content. This is also an effective way to attract more readers, social media followers and subscribers.

10. Memes

Admit it, we have all shared memes that have made us laugh or touched us deeply. Memes are not just great for social sharing but also help your readers take a breather from more long-winded and serious content, and look at the lighter side of a situation.

Memes can be made without much time or effort using resources such as Meme Generator or Quick Meme. They can be customized for any subject or industry. If you want to put your point across in a smarter and more light hearted way, memes are the way to go.

Of course, they cannot be standalone pieces of content on your blog. However, they can be used for gaining some social media traction or complementing text posts.

To avoid any miscommunication or controversy, ensure that you do a little background research to understand the connotations attached to different characters and what they stand for. Do not blindly lift images to create memes without understanding the attached significance. The last thing you want is a backfired effort.

11. Interviews

Interviews are another great way to impress your audience. The more authoritative and influential your interviewee, the better it is for your blog credibility. Your followers/readers can learn a lot when it comes straight from the horse's mouth. Pick an important figure within your industry, and get them to feature for a full-length interview on your blog.

You can either do a video interview, a live podcast or send a list of questions for the person to answer in a textual format. Look at Mixergy for instance. The site is dedicated to interviewing accomplished people.

How do you go about conducting an interview?

Begin by introducing the expert. Highlight their accomplishments to make the prospect of listening to them attractive for readers.

Prepare a list of questions in advance by doing some background research about the experts. Of course, follow up questions will pop up throughout the interview. However, a set of prepared questions will lend it a structure. Conclude the interview by doing a quick summary of all the interesting and important things discussed in the interview. Offer your audience/readers a clear takeaway. Make a conclusion more urgent and actionable.

12. Printable Check Lists and To-Do Lists

This one sure makes the life of your readers easier by compiling all the scattered tasks or items into a single, organized list. It ensures that a task is done more efficiently, and nothing is left out. Wedding checklists, travel checklists, new baby checklists, blog creation checklist, etc., are extremely popular among their target audience.

Give your readers the option of saving these checklists in a printable PDF format. Checklists are great when it comes to getting readers to sign up for your mailing list.

13. Videos

Videos are a brilliant way to make your content both appealing and informative to your readers. Multiple studies have pointed to the fact that people register things more powerfully when they see it being done than simply reading about it.

Visuals strike a chord with your target audience and add variety to your content strategy. Social is becoming increasingly visual in nature. It is all about eye-catching visuals and slickly packaged, easy-to-follow videos. Also, YouTube is the world's second most widely used search engine, which gives you a fair idea about the amount of video content people are consuming.

Make videos that show off your blog's/brand's personality. It does not cost a lot to make basic, good quality videos. Use a smart phone for capturing a video, along with an editing software tool such as Camtasia.

Experiment with multiple video formats like screencasts (talking into the camera), fast paced videos or explainer videos. Keep it short, power-packed and to the point, since people do not really have the time to view videos that ramble endlessly. Plus, putting up your video on YouTube boosts your social signal with Google, who sees all the engagement as a validation of your content and popularity among readers.

Pro Tip: Give your videos a more well-rounded context by including a blog post or a video transcript (that viewers can later refer).

14. Spotlight Posts

People love human interest stories that relate to other people. When you create personal spotlight posts, you instantly engage followers emotionally. It makes the content more interesting and digestible for people. For instance, you can create a behind the scenes story featuring your employees or clients.

Make your blog more personal by showing your audience how it works. It will invariably make your brand appear more human, identifiable and approachable.

Alternatively, you can take advantage of a personal spotlight post by interviewing someone in or out of your company. This is especially beneficial if you can wrangle someone with a recognizable name, but this is not a necessity.

Personal spotlight posts can be beneficial in making you seem more personal, but they should not constitute the majority of your campaign. Use them as a complementary element of your strategy, serving as an occasional alternative-style post. Also be sure to rotate the subject of your post, or else your readers could get bored.

Chapter Five:

10 Content Marketing Tips to Take Your Blog into the Next League

Now that we know why content creation is so integral to the process of creating profitable blogs and how to create stellar content, let's look at how you can widen your reach and draw an even bigger audience to your blog by using these highly actionable content marketing strategies.

1. Guest Blogging

One of the easiest and most effective ways to spread the word about your blog and come off as more authoritative at the same time is to write guest blog posts. You find similar blogs in your niche or popular industry websites and create insightful posts for them.

Make it well-researched, detailed and analytical to position yourself as an expert on the subject. You will not just end up building brand authority but also draw a swarm of traffic to your blog. Include a link to your blog in the author bio along with a power-packed description.

2. Social Media Ads

Social ads are a good way to gain some traction for your posts. You do not need to throw away hundreds of dollars on promoting your blog. Even a post boost of $15-20 can help you gain decent exposure if you have put out amazingly share-worthy content. Ads (especially Facebook ads) give you a very large yet focused audience.

3. Do not Be Overtly Promotional

Do not be overtly promotional when it comes to content marketing. Remember the purpose is to take your reader/potential buyer through a buying cycle. Do not go full throttle, jet boating on your customers immediately. Let them gain some value before you start seeking conversions.

4. Start with a Framework

You may not always have products or services to talk about, especially in the earlier stages of the blog. Skip the product/service talk and focus on a larger framework (that impacts readers) that deals with themes, ideas and issues. Keep the topics closely connected and relevant to your target audience.

5. Do not Monetize Until You Rank

Garnering links to your posts can be really tough. Make it simpler by not combining your content marketing (drawing an audience to your blog) with monetizing efforts. Do not undertake any money making activity until you rank well. Once you have undertaken sufficient outreach activities, rank well, and draw a decent audience of regular readers, only then start your monetization methods. Do not ruin your blog's long term chances by trying to make a few quick bucks from your blog early on.

Of course, you may not have the luxury to wait until you make money. People need quick returns to meet their expenses. If you can afford to hold off earning from your blog (until you rank well for competitive keywords and draw a decent traffic), you can gain a lot more in the long run.

6. Leverage Email Campaigns

Much as new-age internet marketers would have you believe otherwise, email campaigns are far from dead. Emails continue to play a vital role in the process of generating traffic for your blog.

Send interesting, informative and content rich newsletters to your email subscribers. Integrate content into a logical sales funnel that compels your target audience to buy. For instance, if you are selling some products related to baby nutrition, try to offer some tips or recipes related to nutrition.

Establish your expertise in the field of child nutrition, and get readers to trust you by populating their email feed with valuable and useful content.

7. Connect with Influencers

Create a list of influencers within your industry using a tool like Little Bird. Use social media to connect with them. Cross promote each other's blogs. Retweet the content of popular influencers for them to notice you and follow your blog, and eventually share your content among their followers.

Get them to write guest posts for you and share links to the post on their social media pages. This way their hundreds of followers will find you and start following you too.

8. Create Evergreen Content

Evergreen content are pieces that stay relevant irrespective of its time of publication. You can create tons of free how-to guides and small reports that remain relevant to your audience, which saves you the hassle of updating the content periodically.

9. Use Your Best Headlines for Pay Per Click Ads

If you are using PPC campaigns to promote your blog, repurpose your best-performing headlines into an attention-grabbing ad copy. If you realized that a headline worked particularly well with your target audience, repurpose into your ad copy. There really isn't much difference between blog post content and PPC ads regarding the angles that are used to hook readers/customers (such as emotionally tugging angles, strong action verbs, and clear benefits). If you are not sure between different set of headlines, run A/B test to gauge how each headline is performing individually. You will know what types of headlines or content ad copy resonates best with your audience.

10. Keep it Consistent with Your Brand Voice

Content marketing is the best way to develop, refine and reinforce your brand/blog's voice. However, even the biggest brands fail to identify their voice or clearly define it.

Ensure that your content reflects the consistency and continuity of your brand. Review your editorial stands periodically to ascertain that the tone and voice of your brand are consistent with the blog persona in general. Are you positioning yourself as a fun, youthful, fresh blog for a younger audience? Are you positioning yourself as an authoritative and serious source of information in your industry?

While drafting or marketing each post, ask how the content can advance you blog's persona, goals or value? What does the tone of your blog reflect? Does it reinforce your company's values?

11. Answer Complex Questions Using Long Tail Keywords

Attempt to answer complicated questions related to your niche with more targeted and specific, long-tail keywords. You will increase your chances of ranking for a larger number of more focused keywords, where customers are actively seeking information.

While some content creators and marketers believe in writing naturally without adopting a keyword based approach, others strongly advocate targeting your audience with long tail or more focused keywords. Before creating content that you are using for boosting your content marketing efforts, make a comprehensive list of the keywords you are looking to rank for.

By doing a quick scan or survey of some popular forums within your industry, you will know exactly what your readers are looking for. Make dedicated and detailed posts for addressing these queries, and post them of these forums (if permitted). You can also leave lots of smart tips or ideas or little-known information on these forum threads and include a link to your blog in the author bio.

Conclusion

Thank you for downloading my eBook *Blog Writing: The content creation blueprint (how to master content creation to propel your blog on to the next level and make even more serious money online)*.

I sincerely hope the book was able to help you gain insights into the process of content creation for running a highly profitable blog.

The next step is to stop planning and start taking action. There are tons of little-known tips, tried and tested strategies and actionable wisdom nuggets for helping blog publishers build their blog content, increase their authority and establish an equation of trust with potential buyers. From beginners to seasoned blog publishers and marketers, everyone can benefit from the easy-to-follow yet insanely effective strategies discussed in this book.

Finally, if you enjoyed reading the book, please take some time out to share your thoughts by posting a review on Amazon. It would be highly appreciated.

Here's to being a highly successful blog publisher!

Blog Writing:

Advanced Strategies to Monetize Your Blog

Anthony James

© Copyright 2018 by Anthony James

All rights reserved.

The following eBook is reproduced below with the goal of providing information that is as accurate and reliable as possible. Regardless, purchasing this eBook can be seen as consent to the fact that both the publisher and the author of this book are in no way experts on the topics discussed within and that any recommendations or suggestions that are made herein are for entertainment purposes only. Professionals should be consulted as needed prior to undertaking any of the action endorsed herein.

This declaration is deemed fair and valid by both the American Bar Association and the Committee of Publishers Association and is legally binding throughout the United States.

Furthermore, the transmission, duplication or reproduction of any of the following work, including specific information, will be considered an illegal act irrespective of if it is done electronically or in print. This extends to creating a secondary or tertiary copy of the work or a recorded copy and is only allowed with express written consent from the Publisher. All additional right reserved.

The information in the following pages is broadly considered to be a truthful and accurate account of facts and as such any inattention, use or misuse of the information in question by the reader will render any resulting actions solely under their purview. There are no scenarios in which the publisher or the original author of this work can be in any fashion deemed liable for any hardship or damages that may befall them after undertaking information described herein.

Additionally, the information in the following pages is intended only for informational purposes and should thus be thought of as universal. As befitting its nature, it is presented without assurance regarding its prolonged validity or interim quality. Trademarks that are mentioned are done without written consent and can in no way be considered an endorsement from the trademark holder.

Introduction

Congratulations on downloading this book and thank you for doing so.

The following chapters will discuss advanced strategies on how best to monetize your blog for maximum earning potential and will cover areas which include tips and strategies, how to monetize your blog through advertising, coaching services, affiliate marketing and more.

You will also discover the importance of content delivery on blogs and why and how the right content can go a long way to helping you generate the most income out of your blog. Learn about sponsored posts and what they can do to help you along your way to making your blog a steady income stream as you make your way through this book.

There are plenty of books about this subject on the market. Thanks again for choosing this one! Every effort was made to ensure it is full of as much useful information as possible. Please enjoy!

Chapter 1: Advanced Strategies to Monetize Your Blog

When you first start out on your blogging venture with the aim of making money from your blog, it can seem like a daunting task when there's an abundance of information, and you have no idea where to even begin or how to sift through this myriad of information that is presented to you. To put it simply, making money from a blog is not as hard as you may think, but it is also not as simple as you may think because it is going to require a lot of time, effort, persistence and hard work before you finally see things paying off. And it is not going to happen overnight either if that is what you are hoping.

Monetizing your blog is easy in the sense that you do not need to fork out huge sums of capital up front, and you do not need to be a whiz or a genius that is an expert to get started. Anyone from any field can get started making money from a blog if they know the right way to do it. Monetizing a blog is not easy in the sense that it is going to need you to invest a lot of your time, effort, determination, and you would need to be consistent with these efforts and persevere especially when it seems like things are not moving fast enough, or not moving at all. To successfully make money from your blog, these are the traits you are going to need if you want to make it in this competitive field. Yes, it is competitive because there are literally thousands of blogs online and the numbers just keep growing every year. It is easy to get lost in a sea of blogs and never get yours noticed unless you are equipped with the right strategies to do so.

To make money from your blog, you need to be in it for the long haul. And when you are on the journey to making money from your blog, one thing you should always remember is to not ignore the fundamentals of online marketing. Because making money from your blog at the end of the day is about how well you market your blog.

Once you are ready to start making some serious cold, hard cash from your blog, there will be five rules of blogging that you will need to keep in mind if you want guaranteed success. These rules are the fundamentals to blogging successfully, and if they are not taken seriously, it is going to be almost impossible for you to make money from your blog successfully and you will just end up very disappointed.

Here are five fundamentals of successful blogging that will help you make an income from your blog:

- **Deliver Content of Quality** - Nobody is going to be interested in your blog if the content is mostly frivolous. Quality is key to keeping an audience, and blogs with the highest audience traffic are going to have the best success rate to earning an income from the blog. Think about creating content that adds value to the user, and you will have a higher success rate in monetizing your blog.

- **Deliver Content of Value** – Tied closely with quality, your readers need to find your blog valuable. The best way to add value to your readers is to create content that is informative, with video tutorials where possible.

- **Be Focused** – It is of the utmost importance that blogs be focused. Do you have a specific niche or topic that you are really good at? If you do, make that the focus of your blog. Blogs work best when the author knows what they are talking about and that is how you garner a loyal following. If you are not already focusing on a niche, you should be, or you will risk losing your audience. That will do nothing towards helping you earn an income from your blog.

- **Be an Authority** – Similar to having a blog with a focus, a blog with authority is what is going to help you monetize it quicker. Are you an expert at something? Or well-known in your field? That could be a huge advantage to your blog and it will help to drive traffic much faster towards your blog. If you already have authority, all you would need to do is leverage that to your advantage to generate an income stream from your blog eventually.

- **Be Engaging** — Does the kind of content you produce on your blog entice people to spend time reading it? A blog that generates little engagement has very little chance of monetizing the blog. Each piece of content that you produce on your blog should be able to engage and capture the attention of the audience you are targeting, especially if you are selling a product or a service, because your audience will be more likely to make purchases from you that way.

Strategies to Monetizing Your Blog

As with everything else, the secret to success when it comes to monetizing your blog lies in the kind of strategies you employ to help you reach your goals. Here are some excellent strategizing methods that you can utilize to help you make the most out of your blog, which we will discuss in further detail in this book:

- **Email Marketing** — One of the best ways to make money through your blog is email marketing. Email marketing is done through building a list of subscribers which can be added to your email list and then using this list to alert them as to what is the latest that is happening on your blog. Building a list can help monetize your blog by keeping those who are already interested in the know, so they can be the first ones to pick up on any offerings from your blog.

- **Google AdSense** – The easiest way to explain how this works is, you make money by putting ads on your blog. You will earn from Google AdSense based on impressions (which depends on page views) and based on the number of clicks (based on how many visitors click the ads on your page). How much you make on AdSense would depend on the volume of traffic you get to your blog and how many visitors are willing to click the ads that are on your blog.

- **Affiliate Marketing** – This is simply another form of performance-based marketing. This works by including links to a product or service which is offered by another business through an affiliate program on your blog. When choosing an affiliate program, only promote material that is relevant to your niche, products or services that you have personally used and would recommend. Also, do not forget to add a disclaimer to your site.

- **Offer Courses or Services** - Another great tool to generating an income out of your blog would be to create a chance for your viewers to get an exclusive one-of-a-kind opportunity that they may not be able to score elsewhere. The earning potential here would depend on how much people are actually willing to pay for the courses or services that you are offering. It is a great way to generate traffic to your blog.

- **Paid Reviews and Banner-Ads** – You will also be able to generate an income from your blog through paid reviews, sponsored posts and banner ads. Blogs that generate enough online traffic are more likely to be approached by businesses who would be interested in sponsoring your blog.

- **Securing Sponsorships for Your Blog** – To be able to garner sponsorships, your blog needs to be generating a high volume of traffic to make a significant amount of money successfully. Sponsorship is a great tool for making money if you are using it right. With sponsorship, always be upfront with your readers and audience and be as transparent as possible, so you are not misleading them in any way.

While there are more ways than one to generate an income from your blog, the methods listed above are among the core methods that will see the fruition of all your hard work.

Chapter 2: Making Money Through Advertising on Your Blog

Monetizing your blog is going to require quite a bit of effort, and one of the ways to generate an income is through advertising. Advertising here can include sidebar ads, in addition to your average standard ad that you see on blogs which are already making money.

What You Need to Consider Before Joining an Ad Network

There is only one reason you would join an ad network – to make money, of course. But before you go jumping into all sorts of ad networks in an attempt to make the most money out of your blog, there are a couple of things which you are going to need to consider here:

1. Will the ad network be able to offer you the guaranteed CPM rate you are after? Be mindful of the fact that many ad networks are guilty of enticing new or struggling bloggers with promises of great returns, but remember that if an offer sounds too good to be true, then it probably is.

2. Do you have a contract? An agreement in black and white is always the way to go, and if

an ad network is reluctant to offer you a concrete agreement, best to walk away from it to avoid finding yourself getting stuck in a bad situation.

3. Will you have any sort of control over the ads that are run? Ideally, the ads that are going to be featured on your blog should be in sync with the content that is being talked about on your blog. You do not want an ad that is in contrast to your content because it is going to send mixed messages to your readers and your blog runs the risk of losing credibility among your followers. When signing up with an ad network, get it in writing that you have the right to request any ads you deem inappropriate for your blog to be removed without issues.

Joining an ad network has its pros and cons. Ad networks basically work like advertising brokers, whereby you offer an available advertising space on your blog for purchase, and they will do their part trying to sell the space for you for a cut of the sale.

The pros of working with an ad network are:

- There is less effort on your part in the sense that you are not stuck being a one-person show doing all the legwork selling and setting up your advertising. By joining an ad network, all you have to do is sign a contract and place an HTML code on your sidebar, and you are set.

- Ad networks can sometimes earn more than private advertising can, although how much you make would vary depending on several factors.

- Ad networks do more than just sell ads since they work with multiple bloggers and have more connections. They can attract a bigger pool of prospective clients, some of which may have big advertising budgets they can work with, an opportunity that may otherwise be harder to score if you were working on your own.

And now, the cons of working with an ad network:

- You may not have as much control over the ads as you would like. Ad networks are often reluctant to relinquish control over the ads that get displayed to the blogger, although there are some exceptions. Do not work with an ad network unless you are prepared to give up control and let them have full run of the kind of advertisements that show up on your blog.

- It may be difficult to secure an ad network to work with. Getting in with a network could require months of pushing and persistence.

Having connections and contacts in this instance would definitely give you a leg up. Otherwise, it can be a challenge getting in immediately with these networks and very often you may find yourself waiting for months before an opportunity shows up.

How to Sell More Sidebar Ads

Average advertising is easy enough, and noticeable. It is the sidebar ads that very often go unnoticed in most blogs. But sidebar ads also have earning potential for your blog, so they should not be ignored. One great thing about selling sidebar ads is that you have complete control over the ads that get displayed on your blog at all times, which may not necessarily always be the case with regular advertising through an ad network.

So, how do you get the most out of your sidebar ads? By following these simple rules for monetization:

- **Emphasize on Making It Obvious** – If an advertiser is looking to advertise on your blog, they may not notice that there is an option to advertise on your blog unless you make it loud and clear to them, plain and simple. Make it clear that you have advertising spots for sale by putting an advertisement tab in your header, for example, that will link advertisers to your advertising page. Remember a lot of these advertisers are most likely very busy people who simply do not have the time to comb and sift through your blog wondering if there is any advertising opportunity available. It is up to you to make it obvious.

- **Clarity on Your Advertising Page** – Once you have directed advertisers to your advertisement page, make things even simpler for them by being as detailed as you possibly can. Typically, the kind of information that advertisers would be after include page views and unique visitors to your blog, what your blog's demographics are, and what are the advertising options and prices they can expect. And if you have any testimonials from former advertisers who have worked with you before? Even better! Throw that into the mix too, because it adds credibility to your blog. List down every compelling reason you can think of as to why advertisers should choose to work with you and you will be in business in no time.

- **Offer Special Rates** – Nobody can resist a good discount or a bargain. If you want more advertisers to sign up with your sidebar ads, offer them a deal that they simply cannot refuse. For example, offer your sidebar advertising rates at 50% off the original price. Limited time offers are a great gimmick to entice these advertisers to sign up for your deal, and they will be a lot keener to take up a sidebar ad subscription on your blog if they feel that they are getting a bang for their buck.

- **Throw in an Extra Treat or Two** – Companies love feeling like they are getting the most out of their money, and sidebar advertising is a great opportunity to make the companies who work with you feel special. Seal the deal with your new partners by offering to mention the company on your Facebook or Twitter accounts for example, which is a free form of publicity for the company. You could even offer to write a free blog post for the company if you love what they are selling and you are comfortable promoting their products or services to your readers.

- **Do not Leave Blank Spots** – If your sidebar ads are empty, it gives the impression that your blog space is not quite up to par yet for people to want to advertise on your blog. This could be the kiss of death for your money generating attempts, so avoid leaving blank ad boxes even if you do not have any ad deals signed up. Fill those spots with affiliate ads or work with friends who run their own blogs and give them free advertising for example. Anything to keep up the appearance that your blog is interesting enough to advertise upon and this will, in turn, attract other advertisers if they see there is already an interest built on your blog.

Chapter 3: Monetizing Through Product Creation

Aside from earning money through advertising, make the most out of your blog by offering products and services that your readers will not be able to score elsewhere. When a product or service is offered exclusively, your earning potential increases because readers will only have to come to your blog to get what they want. Even better if you are an authority in your field and they know that what they are paying for is going to add value and be well worth it. An example of how to make the most money out of your blog would be through creating and selling online courses, selling products or services, and organizing giveaways.

Creating and Selling Online Courses
The first question you may ask is, why would readers pay for an online course? One reason – because the course is teaching them something they need to know. And let's face it, online learning is big these days, thanks in large part to how convenient it is to learn something from the comforts of home and at your own pace. If you are an expert on a subject, consider creating an online course on your blog.

When creating an online course, it is best to focus on a specific subject or topic at any given time. Online courses hold more value than your average blog posts because of the teaching quality involved, and the opportunity your readers are getting to learn something of value that they could make use of for the money that they are paying.

To successfully create an online course that is going to help generate income for your blog, you would want to keep these helpful pointers in mind:

- **Include the Two "I"s in Your Course** – The two "I"s, in this case, would be informative and inspirational. This is the most important criteria that you are going to need to encompass into your blog. Otherwise, you would just be wasting everyone's time, and your readers are going to become disenchanted with your blog. Share information that is based on facts, and create a course that is going to inspire your readers into action once the course is over. Being informational will set your blog apart because your readers will come to know that your blog is the one to go to if they want to learn something useful. Being inspirational with your posts, ideas and sharing personal experiences, which you can incorporate into your course, will inspire your readers into believing that they can do it too.

- **Be Clear with Your Objectives and Focus** – If you intend to monetize your blog, this is another big factor you are going to want to pay attention to. If you can create a course that is niche, focused and targeted to a specific group where there is a demand, that immediately increases your chances of monetization right there. You need to offer a course that makes your readers feel they NEED to be a part of this or they will be missing out on something important. That they NEED your course because it holds the answers to everything they need to know.

- **Price Your Course Reasonably** – Everyone wants to make as much money as they possibly can, but let's not get carried away here. To really draw your audience in, you are going to need to offer a course that is fair enough to compensate for your time and effort, but at the same time not priced too high that your target audience is going to feel it is way out of their budget and price range to take part in the course. If you can offer the course at a discount, especially if it is your first online course, that would be even better.

Selling Products, Services and Organizing Giveaways

If you have a passion or skill for something, consider offering that service, skill or product on your blog. Selling a skill, service, or product that your readers need will cement your blog's reputation as the go-to blog for what they need. This is turn will drive a higher volume of traffic towards your blog which helps with the advertising aspect of it, so really it is a beneficial situation on many levels.

Giveaways are also another method of generating an income from your blog. Depending on the nature of your blog, research some companies that you can potentially work with, approach them and see if they would be interested in a product giveaway collaboration with your blog. If you are a beauty blog for example, and you have posted about reviews about your favorite makeup or skincare brands on your blog, consider approaching those companies for a possible opportunity. Convincing companies to collaborate with you on your blog is not as hard as it may seem, the key is to convince them why it would benefit their company to be working with you.

Selling products, services, and organizing giveaways are a great way to generate traffic to your website and if your readers like what you are pitching, they are more likely to buy from you, and keep revisiting your blog many times over.

Chapter 4: Monetizing Your Blog Through Affiliate Marketing

Affiliate marketing is another great tool to maximize the earning potential from your blog. Commonly mistaken for referral marketing, affiliate marketing is a form of marketing known as performance-based marketing, and how it works is a business will reward one or several of its affiliates for each visitor or customer that the affiliates bring in through their own efforts. Bloggers who have been around for a while know that affiliate marketing too has been around for years and they know full well that this form of marketing is one of the most lucrative ways for a blog to earn money online.

Affiliate marketing is one of the oldest forms of marketing around, and one of the most effective methods that benefit the readers while helping your blog make money at the same time. Bloggers make money by building an audience base that stays loyal to the blog by offering products, services or courses that will benefit the audience and help them in a way that they need. Affiliate marketing is merely a faster way to offer products or services without the blogger having to create those products and services from scratch. As a blogger utilizing affiliate marketing, all you have to do is introduce your audience to certain products or services (from companies that you trust and can vouch for regarding effectiveness), and you get a commission on any sales that occur from the marketing efforts on your blog.

Still not convinced how affiliate marketing can help? Five compelling reasons are all you need to see why affiliate marketing is the direction you need to head towards if you are serious about monetizing your blog:

1. You come to know what your audience really wants, what services or products they are after so you have a better idea of what you may be able to offer in the future should you wish to branch out on your own.

2. Affiliate marketing monetizes your blog much faster than it would if you were to create your own product from scratch which could take a considerable amount of time depending on what you are offering.

3. You become known among your readers as a trusted authority, and they become accustomed to buying from you. Provide excellent service and honest reviews, and your readers will have no qualms about buying from you in the future when you someday launch your own products or services.

4. It is easy to implement. Enough said.

5. You do not need to be a specialist or an expert to get on board with affiliate marketing, all you need to be is familiar enough with what you are marketing.

How to Maximize Your Earning Potential Through Affiliate Marketing

Ready to start including affiliate marketing as part of your advertising efforts? Take a look at these tips below to help you maximize the earning potential you can get out of your affiliate marketing efforts:

- **Stick to Your Values** – Never compromise your values for the sake of making a quick buck. Always be honest and never give a review that you do not fully believe in yourself if you want to retain credibility among your readers. Yes, affiliate marketing is a great tool to make use of, but only align yourself with products or services that you genuinely love and would recommend to someone else. Ask yourself if you would be willing to refer this product for free, even if you were not being paid for it. If you answer is yes, then go ahead.

- **Make Honesty Your Best Policy** – If your readers feel that they can trust you, they are more likely to stay loyal and buy what you are offering. Never promote a product or service that you do not absolutely love yourself or something that you do not fully believe in. As a blogger who is serious about making an income from your blog, you need to practice transparency all the time and build your reputation around being a credible, reliable and trustworthy source.

- **Direct Promotion** – Instead of promoting your affiliate products or services on the sidebar ads on your blog, consider promoting a product or service directly in a post itself because it garners more attention that way. Include it in a product or service review for example, with as much detail as possible, enough to convince your readers that they should buy the product or service too.

- **Do not Go Overboard** – It is easy to get excited about things that can help you make money, and while it may be tempting to include as many affiliated links on your blog as possible to get the most money out of it, in this instance less may be more. Choose your affiliate links carefully and strategically – this is a much more effective approach than bombarding your blog with dozens of links that are all over the place. Ideally, select affiliates that are in line with the vision and the voice of your blog, your readers will believe an endorsement more if they.

- **Learn the Ropes** – Do not be discouraged by the fact that in affiliate marketing, you are going to have to experiment a little to see what works and what does not. Some may work better than others, but the key is to be persistant until you find what works best for you. Each experience will bring you closer to understanding what your readers want and expect, all of which can prove to be useful information for the future of your blog.

- **Never Cut Corners** – Your relationship with your blog's audience is your most important asset, one that you should never lose. Your readers and your audience are the lifelines of your blog, without them, there is no possibility of maximizing the full earning potential from your blog. Having said that, a blogger should never betray the confidence of their audience and readers for the sake of making money through affiliate marketing, because you risk losing more than just your audience in the long run. Always remind yourself before working on any affiliate marketing efforts that this should improve the relationship between the blog and its readers, not the other way around.

Chapter 5: Monetizing Your Blog Through Coaching Services

Contrary to what you may think, you do not have to be blogging for years or to have massive amounts of experience before you can attempt to offer coaching services through your blog. What makes coaching such an in-demand thing is that your readers will inevitably be facing all sorts of challenges at some point in their life. Everyone has their own challenges that he or she need to overcome, and coaching is a positive way to help your readers through that period in his or her lives when they may need it the most. And that is something they would be willing to pay money for.

Coaching is a great tool to use on your blog if you are serious about making money from it. It is common for bloggers to dabble in online coaching these days, and coaching is a great way to nurture a loyal audience following. Why would your audience be keen on coaching services if you were to offer them on your blog? Because of the results that they hope to achieve through that coaching. As a coach, your focus should be on helping your readers to deal with the challenges in their lives positively and constructively to help them overcome the hurdles that they may find impossible to do on their own without a little help.

One of the great things about coaching is the endless possibilities and the many areas that you can delve into. You could opt for life coaching, business coaching, skills coaching, career coaching, performance coaching, executive coaching and much more depending on what you are best at. The most important thing is to convince your readers why your coaching program is better than anyone else's and why they should sign up with you instead.

Why Coaching and How Can It Make Money for My Blog?

Coaching for some is a rewarding experience because they derive pleasure in knowing that they have helped someone else solve a problem or be better at a certain task they were struggling with. Coaching is for some, a way for them to help others and in the process, sharpen their skills at solving a problem while building their reputation as the person to go to if someone were to have a similar problem.

If coaching is something you are great at doing and you already have a blog that has been around long enough to develop a loyal following, take the opportunity to dive into coaching and help make an even bigger impact in the lives of your readers. People are always looking for a solution to their problems and help where they are struggling, and this is something they will be willing to pay for, which makes it a great monetizing opportunity. Coaching on your blog is a great way to strengthen your relationship with your readers who in turn, could draw in more potential readers to your blog which equals more traffic. More traffic at the end of the day means more advertising opportunity, which in turns helps your blog become a money generating machine in the long run that can churn out money for you even while you are sleeping. If your readers like what you are selling, they will buy from you, there is no doubt about that.

Coaching helps your readers, but it also helps you as a blogger at the same time. The whole point of starting a blog in the first place is because you have a passion for something, and a desire to share that information and knowledge (especially if you are an authority on it) with the rest of the world. Coaching is just taking it to the next level where you directly reach out to your readers in an attempt to help them instead of just posting weekly blog posts and updates. Blog posts and articles are speaking to the general audience, but when you offer to coach, suddenly it becomes much more personal. Addintionally, if your readers already like what they have seen on your blog thus far, they will not hesitate to pay for any coaching programs you offer if they feel they stand to benefit from it.

The best part about coaching through your blog? Your earnings are not limited by your geographical location. Because it is online, you have the potential to reach people from across the globe, which means your earning potential skyrockets just like that. If you are good, people will be willing to pay.

How to Get Started with Coaching on Your Blog

The first thing you need to do if you want to offer to coach on your blog is to establish the niche you are coaching for. A coaching program that a reader is going to be most enticed towards is one that highlights the aspects of a situation that the reader is going through and that they need help with. To do that, the coaching program offered on your blog needs to be specialized in solving specific problems that your readers have, only then will they be willing to pay money for your program.

The second thing you need to do to establish a successful coaching program that is going to help you generate an income from your blog is to identify what kind of coaching structure you are going to go for. Are your sessions going to be solely blog based? Would you offer a live video session on your blog that your readers can tune into? Would you be holding your coaching sessions in person in a specific location? Either method you choose, your readers should only be able to sign up for your coaching sessions through your blog, as that is how you will be able to generate an income from it. Coaching through your blog would definitely be the easier option as all your readers would need is a good internet connection. They do not have to waste time commuting back and forth, do not have to sit in traffic and they have the flexibility of tuning in to your coaching sessions when it is convenient for them.

Create a coaching program that is ongoing, so your readers will always keep coming back to your blog. An ongoing coaching series has a lot more earning potential than a one-off program. Remember to make your coaching sessions educational, informative, inspirational, and most importantly, offer insightful tips that your readers can employ to their own problems. Create content that is of value to your readers to keep them coming back for more. Teach your readers how to achieve their goals and overcome challenges with constructive tools and advice and your coaching courses will become a hit in no time.

Chapter 6: The Importance of Content Delivery

By now, you should have already come to realize that the success of a blog boils down to the kind of content that is delivered on the blog. For a blog to succeed enough to the level that it can constantly make money, it needs to always be at the top of its game when it comes to content, and mediocre or lackluster content is just not going to cut it. A successful blog is one that delivers content of value to its readers.

The Right Way to Deliver Content on Your Blog for Maximum Earning Potential
Bloggers who make some serious dough with their blogs know the five golden rules when it comes to the kind of content they have on their blog. So, how do you always ensure that the content on your blog is top-notch enough for your blog to become a money generating machine?

1. **By Being Yourself** – Never try to be someone that you are not. A blog that is trying to pretend to be something that it is not is a blog that is never going to get very far, much less make any money from. Remember the reason that you decided to start your blog in the first place - because you have insight, knowledge, or skills that you know could be useful to other people and you want to share

that with the world. So do it! Do not try to copy or imitate other successful blogs because no two blogs are the same. Make your blog your own, be your own person and your content will have a unique voice of its own that is going to resonate with the readers.

2. **By Not Being Fake** – Starting a blog should not be just about making money, you need also to be passionate and love what you are doing if you are going to deliver content of quality. Content that isn't genuine is going to just turn your readers away if they feel that your blog is not genuine enough for them. Loss of audience equals loss of revenue, so if you are going to start a blog, be sure that it is also about the passion and not just about the money. Do what you love, and the money will follow.

3. **By Being Engaging** – The content on your blog should be of an interactive nature, where it encourages your readers to respond with their own comments and reach out to you via the email address listed on your blog. Be an authority that your readers want to reach out for advice and input after reading your blog. Post a variety of different things, share personal experiences, talk about topics from your own point of view, anything that you think will be able to engage your readers just a little bit more.

4. **By Being Confident** – To post content that is worthy and valuable on your blog, you are going to have to be confident about what you are writing about. Do not compare yourself to other writers or bloggers who may seem to post funnier content or content with a more creative flair and style for writing, for example. Constant comparisons and trying to keep up with other bloggers will only serve to make you lose sight of what unique traits you have to offer on your blog, and your content will inevitably suffer because of it. Be confident about what you have to share and let it show in the way you deliver your content, and your audience will respond well to that.

5. **Be Settling for Nothing Less Than Perfection** – The content on your blog is going to be out there for the world to see. And you are going to want to make sure that what they are seeing is nothing short of perfect. As a blogger, you should always be working and striving to improve, not just on your skills as a writer, but in the way you deliver the content before hitting the publish button. Read your post several times over, check for any grammar or spelling errors, eye your content from a critical point of view and ask yourself how this post is going to add value to the person who is reading it. Settle for nothing less than perfect.

Chapter 7: Monetizing Through Sponsored Posts

Sponsored posts are one of the quickest methods of making money from your blog. Sponsored content is content that you are being paid to write or come up with by a company or a brand, which means that the content you create will have to be promoting a particular brand or service offered by the company in question. Sponsored content differentiates itself from marketing through one simple aspect – you are paid for the content you create, as opposed to relying on possibly generating an income based on the number of clicks or sales.

Introducing your readers to new products or services that they may not already be aware of is one way of providing value to your readers, but the trick is here to create content that is top-notch and honest at the same time without compromising the credibility of your blog.

When it comes to sponsored posts, you may be tempted to take on as many as possible because you are guaranteed a payment for each one, but cool your jets and try to avoid doing so, because a blog that has too many sponsored brands can be a turn off for a lot of readers. They will begin to doubt if they can really trust what your blog is saying if they feel you are just creating these sponsored posts for the sake of the money. Be savvy and be smart and selective about the kind of sponsored posts and campaigns you want to take on and limit the number of brands you commit to at any given time. Even though your content is being paid for by the sponsor for you to spin some positive light on it, it should still hold a genuine voice to it and not come across as fake to your readers. Before you hit the publish button, ask yourself - if you were reading your post from a third-party point of view, would it be convincing enough?

What Is the Earning Potential with Sponsored Content?

You need to know what your blog is worth. Earnings from a sponsored post can vary depending on the company and brand in question, but it is also important for you as a blogger to know what the value of your blog is. If your blog has been around for a long time, for example, and has developed a strong following with hits on the site every day, you have more bargaining power which will allow you to negotiate a better deal for your sponsored content.

Why Sponsored Posts Are an Awesome Revenue Generating Tool

With the rise of influencers online, companies realize the value of purchasing sponsored posts and are constantly on the lookout for influencers and bloggers to work with. Having a company featured on a blog is a great way to boost sales, and for this reason, it is a great way for bloggers to take this opportunity to make some money if they have a blog space to offer.

What makes sponsored posts so great is that you do not have to invest too much time or effort into it. In fact, it is quite possibly easier than a lot of other types of campaigns which can be more demanding and cost a lot more money. Sponsored posts are easy. In fact, sometimes all a company needs is a link or a mention of their product or service on existing blog posts or an upcoming blog post that they could pay to be mentioned in.

In contrast with affiliate marketing, one of the most exciting things about sponsored posts for bloggers is that they are paid more or less immediately. This may vary depending on the sponsor in question, of course, as some sponsors will prefer to pay up front and others may opt for payment only after you have published a post on them. Still, it is a lot faster than affiliate marketing and advertising, and the pay here can be pretty good depending on how popular your blog may be and how much traffic it generates on a daily basis. It is a quicker option to monetizing your blog compared to a lot of other monetizing efforts.

How to Secure Sponsored Posts on Your Blog

If you do not already have companies who are queuing up to get sponsored on your blog, then you need to be proactive and start approaching companies that you would like to work with and convince them why it would be a great idea to collaborate with your blog. If you are worried about whether your blog needs to be amazingly popular or have a high volume of traffic before companies and brands will even consider working with you, don't worry. As long as you can produce great content of value, that is going to be what matters the most.

When presenting your pitch to these companies, be specific about what the company or brand can expect if they decide to work with you. Tell them your ideas with enthusiasm and give them as much detail as possible to really show it is going to be well worth their time and money to secure a sponsored post on your blog. Tell them what you plan to write, who your readers are and what they want, how much traffic your blog generates, be as specific as possible and spare no detail.

Do not be afraid to show your creativity when trying to convince companies and brands to work with your blog. Creativity shows that you think outside the box and you are all about ideas. It is ideas with a creative spark that is going to drive an interest towards a product or service. Show the companies or brands that you hope to work with what you can do for them, and they will be more than interested in teaming up with your blog for a sponsored post or two. Maybe even more.

The Types of Sponsored Post Options to Work With

The types of sponsored post options that bloggers would have to work with are sponsored posts that have access to the readers and sponsored posts which are just a link to the blog or website. The type of sponsored content would depend on the company or brand's preference and what they think would work best for them.

Sponsored content that has access to readers would depend on the type of influence your blog has. The more influence a blog has, the more likely the company is to decide on this route when it comes to post sponsorship. Sponsored content that works with just a link would depend on how much authority a blog's domain has. The higher the domain authority, the more opportunities your blog will have. Which is why it is important to pitch as many details as possible about your blog to the company or brand you hope to work with so they can make an informed decision and get the most out of their sponsored post collaboration with your blog.

Chapter 8: Remarketing to Become a Paid Blogger

If you have been running your blog for a while now and you get the feeling that you need to work on re-engaging your readers and visitors to your blog, then you are probably in need of remarketing. Remarketing is also known as retargeting, and quite simply, it is a way to re-engage with your audience and hopefully increase your conversion rates and return on investment (ROI) in the process, especially among viewers who have already visited your blog several times now and are familiar with its contents. Remarketing the right way will make it much easier to convert those readers into customers, thereby making money through your blog.

Is your blog already advertising on Google? If the answer is yes, then you are already halfway there with your remarketing efforts. All you would need to do next is to add a piece of Google's remarketing code (known as a tag or a pixel) to your blog or website. Google's ad retargeting tool is one of the more powerful online marketing tools and techniques, and it works by allowing you to stay connected with your readers and viewers even after they have left your blog. Remarketing has also shown to have much higher click-through and conversion rates than your average ads that get displayed on a blog. If you are seriously considering remarketing yourself to become a paid blogger, this is one way to go about it.

The concept of remarketing is simple enough to understand once you get the hang of it. How it works is when a visitor or viewer browses your blog, they will land on your remarketing list. Once they are done browsing your blog and leave, even if they are browsing different sites on the internet such as Facebook or YouTube for example, they will still be presented with relevant ads for your site which relate to the products or services you are selling or promoting on your blog that they showed an interest in while they were browsing your page. Provided they are on your remarketing list, of course. So, while they may have left your blog, they are still getting little reminders here and there on other sites that indirectly lead them back to your blog. See how that works?

When your viewer has performed a certain pre-defined action on your blog that has been determined by Google Analytics, such as by simply visiting your blog, or browsing through the possible products and services offered, for example, a cookie is placed on the user's browser. From there, it is up to you to analyze the information you have and decide what the next action to take would be that makes the most sense, and what kind of remarketing lists should be created that could better draw in those viewers who could be potential customers with just the right nudge. After all, they have already visited your blog, which means they must be interested in something right?

Back to that cookie that was placed in the user's browser. That cookie will be responsible for making sure the ads will follow the users no matter where they go once they leave your blog. The only catch here is that the ads will only follow the user as long as he or she sticks with using a specific browser. For example, if the user were using Chrome to browse your blog, then the ads would follow the user as long as the user remains on Chrome. And as long as the user does not clear the cache on their browser, you would be able to track the user while they remain on the same browser.

Getting the Most Out of Your Remarketing

To reap the full benefit of remarketing your blog in your efforts to monetize it, it is important to first and foremost, focus on the communication aspect. The importance of tailoring and targeting your communication cannot be stressed enough. Yes, using the same banners and campaign ads may be quicker and more convenient for you, but it will do nothing to help your efforts to really monetize your blog the way you want it to. Tailoring the communication in the way you market your ads for different target audience groups, on the other hand, will bring a much higher chance of engaging a wider audience scope, which guarantees better results. Your viewers and potential readers should feel as if your ads are made specifically for them, and speaking out to them, making them feel as if they absolutely must visit your blog to avoid missing out on something important.

What Are Some of the Remarketing Segments Available?

Within remarketing, there are several different options of visitor types that you as a blogger would be able to work it. The segment types include:

- **Product Specific Viewers** – These encompass the viewers that have already visited your blog and delved into more details about the kind of products or services you have available on your blog. They would be the group that has already shown enough of an interest in the product or service and want to find out more about it. For example, if you were offering coaching services on your blog, they would be the users who are interested enough and possibly want to sign up for a program because they have already spent a certain amount of time concentrating on the service that is offered on your blog.

- **General Viewers** – This could be any viewer who visits your blog, and they could spend anywhere from a minute to several minutes on your blog depending on their interest.

- **Previous Viewers** – Previous viewers are among the groups that should be targeted in your remarketing efforts, especially if they have already visited your blog several times. The interest is already there, they just need the right prompt to convert them into purchasing a product or a service offered by your blog.

- **The Almost-Purchase Viewers** – Encompassed in this group are the viewers who were probably already halfway into purchasing something off your blog, and then at the last minute changed their mind before the final sale could be complete. Pay attention to this group too and find out what can be done to give them the push they need to make the final purchase.

Chapter 9: Monetizing Through Email Lists

Building email lists would be among the common suggestions and advice you would have been bound to come across if you have been studiously researching how best you could make money from your blog. And there's a good reason why. If you are a blogger that is selling a product or service of any kind on your blog, it is imperative that you have an email list or an email newsletter of some sort because it can be a powerful sales tool that you are not taking full advantage of. An email list is a way for you to keep your subscribers updated about the products and services offered on your blog, and more importantly, alert them about any new products or services that are now available. If they do not know about it, how can they purchase it, right?

Being Effective with Email Lists
Being effective with your email lists and the type of information you send out to your subscribers is easy enough. Just ask yourself this one simple question before you hit the "send" button – would I want my best client reading this? If the answer is no, you know what to do. If you are not fully satisfied with it, neither will your readers. Do not send it unless you are sure of it. Remember that the people who are reading your emails are people who could possibly be potential customers if they aren't already, and if you

are serious about monetizing your blog, you are going to need to make your customers your lifeline.

When your readers read your email list, they want to feel that whatever you have put down in there is speaking to them directly, and not just a generic email blast with no specific group or target in mind. Readers like to feel exclusive and special, so make them feel that way and construct your emails like you would as if you were speaking to your readers face-to-face instead of over the internet. Make your reader feel important like you have specifically tailored your product or service to meet their needs, make them feel special and they will keep coming back to your blog for more.

And the most important thing to remember is to always respond to any of your readers who reply to your emails. Always. No ifs, buts or exceptions here. If you ignore your readers, especially when they have personally reached out to you, then the chances of them coming back to you are somewhere along the lines of extremely small and maybe never again. Respond to any emails you will receive from your readers and be prepared to be amazed by how much of a difference that can make, especially on your ROI in the long run.

When crafting your email newsletter, give your readers just enough information and entertainment, but not too much because you want to peak their curiosity enough to redirect them back to your blog if they want to find out more. Remember to be as engaging as possible in your writing, because no reader is going to be interested in reading a dry and dull newsletter that could bore them to tears. Be engaging, be entertaining and be creative.

Building an Effective Email List
With the right strategies in place, you could have your email list up and running in no time. Remember an email list means more blog traffic for you in return, especially if your readers subscribe to your list and keep visiting your blog each time they get an update about something new that is happening on your site. To really maximize on your email list, the following methods will help you give your subscription numbers a boost:

- **Pop-Ups** – Pop-ups are annoying yes, but on some level, they actually do work, especially if the reader is already showing a keen interest in your blog and is a frequent visitor. Many blogs incorporate the use of a pop-up that will encourage the readers to sign up for their newsletter or subscribe to their blog. You have seen it if you have visited other blogs yourself. Annoying at times, yes, but there is a reason many blogs are using this. Because they work.

- **Freebies** – People are sometimes reluctant to give away their email address for fear of being spammed in their inboxes by unwanted emails. Unless... there was a good enough incentive and reason for them to do so. Everyone loves to receive a little gift for free, so why not try that tactic to entice your readers to sign up for your newsletter when he or she visit your blog? Depending on the nature of your blog, try to provide a giveaway that is going to be something of value to your readers, something they would be excited to receive in their inbox. Perhaps a discount to one of your products or services for example.

- **Subscribe Pages** – Your readers cannot subscribe to your blog if there isn't a subscribe page available. To be effective with your subscription pages, it is a good idea to include multiple sign-up boxes for your readers to choose from, and provide the readers with as much detail as possible about what they can come to expect when they subscribe to your blog.

- **Promote Your Blog on Social Media** – It is highly likely that you have your own social media accounts, but are you using these platforms to market your blog? If you are not, then you should! Social media is everywhere, there is no escaping it, so imagine the huge audience potential you are missing out on if you are not leveraging this platform to your blog's advantage. Use your social media account to highlight the exciting features on your email list, update regularly so your social media followers have no chance of forgetting it.

And then we come to the million-dollar question....

How to Monetize Your Email List

By first of all directing traffic to your site. Do you have AdSense on your blog already? Then, you are going to want to tap into the email list potential to get readers heading your blog's way. An email list is an indirect way of monetizing your blog, but you should grab every opportunity you can to link back to your site or even link to a post on your site that has the potential to generate money on its own, then that is what you should do. The more traffic that gets directed to your site, the more potential there is of earning an income from your blog.

The second way is using affiliated links. Do you have a product or service that you are happy with and you have written a shining review about on your blog? Include them in the email that you are going to send out to your subscribers. If your blog has been around for a while, there's going to be a lot of posts and content in it, and sometimes readers just do not have the time to sift through all of that before they find what they are looking for. Why not make things easy for them? Include the affiliate link in that email along with your review, and if the review on your blog is enough to convince them to buy that product or service, you will get a cut of the sale. Money in your pocket, all thanks to your blog and email list.

Do you have a new product or service coming up? Maybe even an eBook? You are going to be glad you have an email list on hand because this is one of the best platforms to start building up an interest among your subscribers before the launch of the new product or service takes place. Ideally, you should start promoting this new release a couple of weeks before it becomes available on your blog, build up an interest and a momentum and get your readers excitedly anticipating for the release so they will not hesitate to buy it once it becomes available. And that is how your email list has just helped you make money through your blog.

Chapter 10: Monetizing Through Pay Per Click

The internet has produced endless possibilities and means of making money, even through blogs and affiliate marketing. Pay Per Click (PPC) is another form of affiliate marketing which can be a great tool for bloggers who are looking to make money online through their blogs. PPC advertising is simple enough to incorporate into a blog. When browsing other blogs, have you ever noticed the ads that are displayed and the side? That is what is known as the PPC ad, and that is what you should have on your blog because each time someone clicks on one of those ads, voila! That is some money in your pocket right there. The amount that you collect from it would depend on several different factors though, such as the industry or the subject of the ad and the blog.

PPC ads have become an increasingly popular way for bloggers to make a little extra money off their blog because of how easy it is and the minimal effort involved. As a blogger, you do not even have to exert any time or energy into hunting for companies who might be willing to advertise on your blog provided that they get a good deal. Google will do it for you through their Google AdSense program, which if you are a blogger you would have no doubt heard about. It is basically easy money in your pocket right there. AdSense allows bloggers to simply insert a HTML code on their website and just like that, the ads will be up and running, ready to make you some extra money each time a viewer clicks on it. An easy enough setup with the potential to help bloggers earn money almost instantly.

When utilizing AdSense, Google will be the one to make the payments per click. The earning potential here would depend on several factors, for example, the more visitors there are to your blog, the higher the chances of having the ad clicked on. And the more people who click on the ad, the more you get paid. Most bloggers can expect to earn anywhere from $0.01 to $1 per click depending on the type of ad and the blog's popularity. The better the blog, the more the earning potential and some ads can even go up to $6 to $7 per click.

Making the Most Out of Google AdSense
How much you can make would depend on one thing – your blog. The more visitors you have coming to your blog, the bigger your earning potential. Bloggers need to invest the time and the effort into creating an amazing and outstanding-looking blog that is chock full of information and engaging material, so much so that viewers will keep coming back over and over and recommend others to your blog. If your readers can engage and connect with your site, there is a higher chance of them clicking on the ads on your site, which is how you are going to make money from it.

Only pack your blog with quality content that is going to add value to your readers, because that is how you keep them coming back. To really make money off of AdSense, you are going to need to drive as much traffic to your blog as possible, and if your readers are not taken with what your blog has to offer, they are not going to keep coming back to it much less spread the word among their connections about your blog. If your content is not engaging enough, directing them to your blog alone will not be enough. The key is to keep your readers on your blog for as long as possible, reading as much as possible. The more they read, the more ads they are likely to see and the better the chances of them clicking on an ad that may be of interest to them.

Not on Google AdSense yet? Get started with a free account today, and you are one step closer to making money from your blog.

Chapter 11: Selling Services & Hosting Virtual Summits

With blogging, the earning possibilities are almost endless if you know how to seize the opportunities when the moments come. There are the direct ways of earning an income through your blog as most of this book has already covered, but there are also the indirect ways of how your blog can help give your income a boost. Here are some ideas of what you can do with your blog that could help put some extra money in your pocket:

- **Produce an eBook** – eBooks are the way to go these days, and it's much easier to produce one now than you may think. Many bloggers are still overlooking the potential that the eBook market holds, and they are probably missing out on hundreds of dollars (or maybe even thousands of dollars) in earning potential every year. As long as you have enough knowledge about a certain subject that people are interested in, and you have enough information to write about, you have everything you need to get started writing your first eBook. A word of advice when venturing into this field is to hire a professional designer for the cover of your book because the cover is going to be the first thing about your book that catches the reader's eye. And no one is going to be interested in a book if the cover alone does not look interesting enough. Write an eBook and market it on your blog, it is a great way to make some money other than what you have already got going on already on your blog.

- **Be a Guest Blogger/Freelance Writer** – If you already have a blog, you probably already have a flair for writing. Why not take the opportunity to use your blog as a springboard for other paid writing opportunities? You double your chances of landing writing gigs and directing traffic to your blog at the same time by including a link to your blog in your application.

- **Do Consultancy** – Bloggers who's blog usually focus on a specific niche subject that they are the most knowledgeable on. Being an authority in your field opens the door of possibility to branching out into consulting services. Consultants and bloggers work the same way – they are experts on a subject matter, and they are helping and guiding other people who need it most. Companies these days are willing to pay bloggers who have proven to be good at what they do and have developed a strong and loyal following to offer consultancy and advice, and this could definitely be an area to look into if you have what it takes.

- **Teach Classes** – Similar to coaching, teaching online courses is another great income generator that could make from your blog. If you already have plenty of success monetizing your blog, why not teach a class about it to other bloggers who may be interested in any advice or strategies for success. Put together a video package and market it on your blog, alert your subscribers about this class through your email lists and social media platforms and if your class is a success, you will be hosting more and more classes before you know it.

Virtual Summits and How They Benefit Your Blog

You have done the advertising, you have done the affiliate marketing, you have done the AdSense, and the eBooks and sold services on your blog. What other way is there to monetize your blog that you have not thought of just yet? How about virtual summits?

If you have never hosted a virtual summit on your blog before, you are going to want to after you read this. Virtual summits are online conferences that bring together a host of experts on a certain subject matter. Viewers get to watch the summits for free for a short period of time, after which they would be required to pay if they want more access and unlimited viewing of the video.

Hosting video summits helps your audience recognize you as the go-to expert and authority in your field as you grow and engage with your audience through engaging and informative content. The right virtual summit video is all you need to turn your followers into customers.

Virtual summits help to grow your email list because if your viewers like what they see, they will want to subscribe to your blog, so they do not miss out on the next video summit opportunity, especially when it is offered free for a certain period of time. Featuring companies and brands on your summit will also help you establish strong partnerships with these companies and brands, and they will be more likely to work with you and your blog in the future.

Hosting allows your viewers to see the person behind the blog, which in turn helps them trust you much quicker than they would by simply just reading your blog or listening to your podcast, for example. People have a higher rate of making purchases from an authority that they trust and respect, and if they can view you along with a panel of other experts who share your same views and opinions on a subject matter, the bond of trust becomes much stronger, and they will be back on your blog for more.

Launching Your Own Virtual Summit
Launching your first virtual summit can seem like a daunting affair, especially when it does not involve just you, but several other individuals as well. A

virtual summit, you need to remember, is an event even if it is conducted online. And like every good event, it needs to be broken down into stages, which makes it much easier to plan and organize. To successfully launch a virtual summit on your blog, here is what you are going to need to do:

- Plan your content. This includes everything from the name of your video, the topic and the theme you plan to cover and down to the last detail of what you and your speakers are going to discuss on the summit. Leave no stone unturned and plan every detail down to the smallest one.

- Prepare the software and hardware you are going to need for your summit, which includes good microphones, webcams, computers and high-speed internet access. In addition to a good location to film your summit of course.

- Reach out to your guest speakers and pitch the idea for your video summit to them and why you would love to get them involved in the project. Aim for many speakers as a summit should ideally consist of anywhere from 20-30 people. Seems like a lot, but once you have built a working relationship with them, it will be easier to get them back again for future summits you may want to host.

- Set up an opt-in page which consists of vital information that will draw your viewers into watching the summit when it is broadcasted. This page should contain pertinent information such as the speakers who will be present, what the topic of the discussion is going to be and most importantly how the viewers will be able to sign up for the summit.

- Prepare an Up-Sell page where your viewers are encouraged to sign up for the all-access pass for unlimited video viewings.

- Record the interviews with your speakers and influencers and embed these interviews on separate landing pages. Be sure to do this only after the agenda for the summit has been prepared, and not before.

- Start promoting your virtual summit on your blog approximately 2-3 weeks before the summit is launched to build up anticipation and a following among your readers. As you draw closer to the date of the summit, increase your promotion of the upcoming event and remind your readers not to miss out on this amazing opportunity.

Conclusion

Thank you for making it to the end of this book. I hope it was informative and able to provide you with all of the tools you need to achieve your goals, whatever they may be.

The next step is to take a look at your current blog and see if enough is being done to maximize its earning potential, and if not, what tips could you make use of from this book that will help you eventually turn your blog into the money-making machine you have always dreamed about. Blogs are a great way to generate an income, and with the right strategies and methods in place, it is now easier than ever to understand what works and what does not when it comes to earning the most out of your blog. Lots of bloggers already have their blogs churning out money for them, and your blog could be next!

Finally, if you found this book useful in any way, a review on Amazon is always appreciated!

Blog Writing:

Traffic Generation Secrets, Hints and Tips

(How to Drive Traffic to Your Blog All Day and Every Day to Gain a Loyal Audience Even While You Sleep!)

© Copyright 2018 by Anthony James

All rights reserved.

The following eBook is reproduced below with the goal of providing information that is as accurate and reliable as possible. Regardless, purchasing this eBook can be seen as consent to the fact that both the publisher and the author of this book are in no way experts on the topics discussed within and that any recommendations or suggestions that are made herein are for entertainment purposes only. Professionals should be consulted as needed prior to undertaking any of the action endorsed herein.

This declaration is deemed fair and valid by both the American Bar Association and the Committee of Publishers Association and is legally binding throughout the United States.

Furthermore, the transmission, duplication or reproduction of any of the following work, including specific information, will be considered an illegal act irrespective of if it is done electronically or in print. This extends to creating a secondary or tertiary copy of the work or a recorded copy and is only allowed with express written consent from the Publisher. All additional right reserved.

The information in the following pages is broadly considered to be a truthful and accurate account of facts and as such any inattention, use or misuse of the information in question by the reader will render any resulting actions solely under their purview. There are no scenarios in which the publisher or the original author of this work can be in any fashion deemed liable for any hardship or damages that may befall them after undertaking information described herein.

Additionally, the information in the following pages is intended only for informational purposes and should thus be thought of as universal. As befitting its nature, it is presented without assurance regarding its prolonged validity or interim quality. Trademarks that are mentioned are done without written consent and can in no way be considered an endorsement from the trademark holder.

Introduction

Congratulations on downloading this book and thank you for doing so.

The following chapters will discuss how to increase the amount of traffic generation to your blog. If you are seeking to make a living (or side cash) from a blog, you definitely need to pay much attention to the amount of and kind of traffic that your blog is generating. Think of it this way: another word for "traffic generation" is "people who are looking at your blog." The more traffic your blog generates, the more money that your blog will make at the end of the day!

Increasing the amount of traffic generation that your blog gets is a labor of love and will take some time. If you want to ensure that you are getting the best kind of attention for your blog and that you can turn that traffic into profit, you have to pursue several avenues of action. Do not expect there to be a single magic pill to get your traffic numbers hiked!

Starting a blog is much like starting a business: it is work! You need to treat your blog the way that you would treat a business. If you go after traffic generation in the right way, you will find that the more work you put into the beginning, the less work that you will need to put in over time. Remember that the Internet never sleeps - it is possible that the work you do during your waking hours will translate into traffic generation while you sleep!

Join us as we explore the ins and outs of traffic generation. While you can certainly use all of the advice in the book, feel free to pick and choose the methods that you think will work best for you. There's more than one way to go after traffic generation! We are here to help you every step of the way.

There are plenty of books on this subject on the market, thanks again for choosing this one! Every effort was made to ensure it is full of as much useful information as possible. Please enjoy!

Part I:

Introduction to Traffic Generation

Chapter 1: What is Traffic Generation

The process of traffic generation is the process of driving unique visitors to your site. In plain English, it refers to actually getting viewers to look at your blog. While many people think that the most difficult part of blog writing is setting up the blog, this could not be farther from the truth. The most difficult part of blog writing is getting the right kind of and amount of traffic generation.

There are thousands of different websites on the Internet that are essentially selling the traffic generation version of snake oil. Many places will say that if you just do this "one neat trick" you will end up with thousands of unique and genuine visitors to your site. Suffice to say that, at best, this is a basket of lies.

Creating unique and worthwhile traffic generation is what will ultimately end up making your blog profitable. How exactly this occurs depends highly on the purpose of your blog. For example, somebody may be using a blog to promote a service or product, while others may prefer to generate their revenue from advertising income. Of course, some blogs have multiple purposes. This book was written from a general perspective; no matter what your vertical is and no matter what your blog focuses on, the advice in this book will apply to you.

If you put enough time and effort into your traffic generation, you will find that it will work for you even when you are not actively sitting at the computer. Some ways of attracting traffic involve physically going out and interacting with other people in your vertical, such as authors of blogs or social media accounts. Others involve working with search engines, a process that is commonly known as SEO, or search engine optimization.

If you think of your blog like a store, consider traffic generation the work you put into getting people coming through the door. After all, your blog has no chance of being profitable if there is nobody looking at it, similar to how a store has no chance to stay afloat if nobody is purchasing its products. Just like there are multiple ways to advertise for stores, there are multiple ways to generate traffic for your blog.

The purpose of this eBook is to introduce you to various ways to promote traffic and generate interest in your blog. With enough hard work and time, you will see that you can attract thousands of quality viewers per day with very little effort.

Chapter 2: Make Sure to Get the Right Traffic

One of the first things it is important to realize is not all traffic generation is the same. Different visitors to your website or blog will have different purposes. Generally speaking, two different kinds of traffic will land on your blog. These two different kinds of traffic are known as "targeted traffic" and "click through traffic."

Targeted traffic is generally considered to be the more "quality" of the two varieties of traffic. Targeted traffic generally knows what it is looking for, and may be specifically looking for the information or product that you are promoting with your blog. For example, if you are writing a blog about budget travel, and somebody enters in "budget travel" to the Google box, they may find your blog. This particular visitor would be considered targeted traffic because they know what they are looking for and found you by using specific terms. Targeted traffic is often found most succinctly by use of appropriate SEO.

Another advantage of targeted traffic is that they know exactly what they are looking for, and thus do not require too much effort to visit your site. The only thing you need to do is make sure that search engines and other advertising avenues understand what it is that your blog is offering.

Click through traffic tends to be a bit more nebulous in nature. Click through traffic is often somewhat hard to measure, as many people will find your blog through random avenues. For example, a popular avenue for click through traffic is the social media website StumbleUpon.

The entire purpose of StumbleUpon is to generate random websites for people to visit as they are surfing the web. If your website is pulled up for a visitor through StumbleUpon, this would be considered click through traffic. They were not specifically looking for the information that your blog has to offer; rather they were simply surfing the web and found you.

Targeted traffic is considered the more valuable of these, as they are more likely to spend more time on your blog. You can examine the average amount of time that people spend on your blog by using an analytics program like Google Analytics. Generally speaking, targeted traffic is going to spend more time reading your content as opposed to click through traffic.

Examining the amount of page time individual visitors have on your website will help you determine what kind of visitor that you are attracting. If your general page time is low, that means that most visitors are clicking on your blog and then leaving it almost immediately. If your general page time is higher, that means that your traffic is spending more time interacting with your content.

Overall, it is much more valuable for you to spend time attracting targeted traffic as compared to click through traffic. The trouble is that targeted traffic can often be a little bit more difficult to win over, as it is less random and many other blogs and websites will be competing for the attention of targeted traffic.

The difference between click through traffic and targeted traffic is why it is very important to understand proper techniques for generating traffic to your website. Many blog owners, who are looking for a quick fix, will often resort to "black hat" traffic generation techniques. These techniques can involve purchasing visitors, or other such tactics designed to make the blog look more popular than it actually is and thus hopefully garner attention from the search engines and, finally, the visitors.

The trouble with these quick fixes is that they are frowned upon by the actual search engines and if you are caught engaging in them, your website may very well be penalized in the rankings. Plus, it is often very obvious to a visitor if a blog has high-quality content on it or not. Blogs with low-quality content will not see very many repeat visitors. Again, if you are treating your blog like a business, you want to create a loyal customer base and keep them coming back. You also want to take advantage of potential word-of-mouth referrals.

One of the most powerful ways to generate traffic is by having your website shared by others. Since this is the Internet, this is most often done through social media, which we will talk about later. If you do not have high-quality content, your traffic will be low quality, and you will end up making very little money.

This is why quality traffic generation will take you some time. You will need to have quality content and make sure that your interactions with your visitors are positive. However, with enough time, you will be seeing the rewards, and your page views will be through the roof!

Part II:

Traffic Generation Tips

Chapter 3: The Importance of Content When Generating Traffic

One of the most important adages in marketing remains true: Content Is King. Particularly if you are looking to make money from a blog, it is very important that the content you have on that blog be worthwhile. Most people on the Internet who read blogs are very well aware of what is good content and what is not. One of the biggest mistakes that prospective blog owners make when it comes to content is by writing more for the search engines than for the reader.

While SEO is certainly important, it should not be outweighed by the importance of your content. It is content that will sell your product, your story, your eBook, or whatever else you are trying to accomplish with your blog. If you want to have a successful blog, you need to have successful content.

What Is Quality Content?

The term "quality content" gets thrown around a lot, but is hardly ever defined. Essentially, "quality content" is something that a reader finds enjoyable to read and also informative. This sounds like it would be a very simple concept, but for many, it is a difficult goal to achieve.

The first thing to ask yourself here is: "Am I a good writer?" Do people honestly enjoy reading what you have to say? If not, you may want to consider hiring a professional copywriter to service the needs of your blog. Many blog owners find this a very worthwhile expense, particularly if they are busy with other projects and do not have the time to spend on generating blog posts day in and day out.

Another thing to keep in mind that "content" does not necessarily have to be limited to the written word. Infographics are very powerful means of communicating valuable information. Many people also have great success with the "vlog," or the "video blog," particularly if you are a person who has a lot of experience in video editing. Producing content in a visual form may be key to generating readership. For example, take popular websites like Buzzfeed. Not only do they have plenty of written media, but they also produce tons of infographics as well as lots of videos. In this way, they can share their content with consumers who may prefer to consume their content in different ways. Not everybody likes reading a blog post. Some people may prefer watching a video.

What Kinds of Content Can I Put on My Blog?

There are many different kinds of content that work well on blogs. You will have to do some experimenting to find the kind of content that you can produce the easiest and get the most returns out of. That being said, these are the most common kinds of content that you will find on successful blogs:

- **Content that educates.** This is a variety of content that is usually backed up by studies and has tons of facts. People who want to learn more about your vertical will often engage with this kind of content. Infographics are a very popular kind of way to display this content.
- **Content that inspires.** This is a kind of content that is generally very shareable in social media and will often give people an attack of the fuzzies. Inspirational content

may involve practical tips as well as more metaphysical inspiration.
- **Content that entertains.** This is probably the most likely of all content varieties to go viral. Something that makes people laugh will definitely make the social media rounds.

To have a successful blog, you will need to find a mix of these three different kinds of content to put into a cocktail that suits your needs best. With the right kind of content, you will attract the right kind of traffic. Nothing brings in excellent traffic like fantastic content.

Make sure that you spend an appropriate amount of time researching your subject before producing your content. A good way to do this is to check out other successful blogs in your vertical. What are they talking about? How are they talking about it? Are their most popular posts actual written blogs, or are they infographics and videos?

Do your research, and you will have excellent content.

Chapter 4: Streamline Blog Design to Bring Traffic

As they say in the entertainment world, appearance is everything. This also applies to your blog. If your blog design is clunky and difficult to use, you will chase off high-quality traffic even before it begins to interact with your great content. You can have the greatest content in the world, but if it is displayed awkwardly, nobody is going to read it.

To help you streamline your blog design to increase traffic generation, we have compiled these easy tips for you.

Make sure that your website is responsive. Your website needs to be easily adapted to several different ways of Internet browsing. For example, if your website does not respond to mobile or tablet devices, that is a huge amount of traffic that you are missing out on. There are several tools on the Internet to determine whether or not Google and other search engines recognize your website as mobile friendly.

Your main blog page should feature snippets of blog posts, not entire blog posts themselves. If you have been blogging with any regularity, you should have scores of different blogs that your potential readers can interact with. It is much more advantageous for you to present your main blog page as snippets of various blogs so that a potential reader can select the topic that they are most interested in. If you only have full blog posts, it is very likely that your visitor will encounter a wall of text, and if they are not interested in that particular blog post, it is likely that they will leave your site.

Use a sans serif font for your blog. A sans serif font is one that does not have lines at the end of the letters. (For example, the font that is being used in this book is a serif font. If you look closely, you will see that there are additional lines marking the ends of the letters.) A sans serif font is easier to read in a blog format.

Use a light-colored background and a dark colored font. This is important because we are accustomed to reading this way. If you read a traditional book, it will have black lettering and a white background. Your blog should be structured in this way. Many people will find a dark background with lighter fonts to be painful on the eyes. Make it as easy for your reader as possible by conforming to traditional reading norms.

Use headers and short paragraphs. A good example of this would be this chapter. At the beginning of each paragraph, there is an attention grabbing sentence that is bolded. The following information is concise and is limited to a few sentences. Walls of text are going to frighten off readers.

Use plenty of images, but preferably not stock photography. Images are a great way to break up walls of text and visually engaging the reader. However, choosing stock photography can be expensive and look cheesy, especially if it is a very popular stock photo that is frequently seen all over the Internet. Just like your content should be uniquely generated, your pictures are better off uniquely generated as well. If you do decide to use stock photography, make sure to use a royalty-free search site or purchase your stock photography. If a stock photography website finds that you have used their images without permission, they can fine you, and you can get into a lot of trouble.

Use social media share buttons to improve the odds of your pieces being shared. People are more likely to share your content on social media if it is easy for them to do so. Make sure to include a reasonable number of social media share buttons at the end of your posts. However, you will want to make sure that they are not obtrusive or overbearing. Just like with traditional advertising, overbearing social media share buttons can be a turn off.

Make sure that your website is optimized for quick loading. This is the Internet. People do not have very much patience. To ensure that your website visitors actually look at your blog, your blog needs to load right away. Many people make the mistake of believing that a beautiful blog design is what will hook readers in. Generally speaking, this is not the case. Of course, you want the blog to look attractive and have the content be easy to read, but you also do not want your visitors to get impatient at the loading time. A perennial example of this is people making use of background images. Background images in a blog bog down the loading time. A better strategy is to use CSS to impart design but also minimize loading time.

Minimize the use of images in your site design. This may seem counterintuitive to the advice given above, but now we are talking about images being used in your actual site design itself. Using background images, as mentioned, is a bad idea because it slows down the loading time. However, this also applies to using image maps as a navigation strategy or using an image as the header of your page. Using too many images in the site design itself will drastically slow your loading time and increase the odds that a potential visitor will leave even before they see your content. Not to mention, image heavy site design is very unfriendly for mobile devices, as the images will not be resized if somebody views your website on a screen with a smaller resolution.

Particularly if you are not a web designer yourself, you may worry about the cost of an efficient and beautiful web design. The good news is that you do not have to be a coding expert to have an efficient and pleasing blog.

There are many websites out there where you can buy flexible and simple web designs for very cheap. For example, if you decide to go with WordPress as your blogging platform, a very popular design is called "Genesis." You can purchase the Genesis framework for a very reasonable price, and then further customize it with add ons. You can even hire professional developers to tinker around with the Genesis framework for a very inexpensive price, as it does not take too much effort for an experienced web designer to make minor modifications to the framework.

Essentially, if you are trying to generate traffic to your blog, you do not want to have your blog design be too complex. A simple and clear blog design that is responsive and easy to read will suit your needs and can be had for a very reasonable price.

Chapter 5: Social Media Matters When Driving Traffic

Social media is one of the most powerful driving forces in traffic generation. Social media is where people go to be, well, social, and if your blog is offering timely or entertaining information, it is likely that people will put it on their social media platform to share.

However, figuring out how and when to use social media can be a very daunting task. There are several different incredibly popular social media platforms out there, and which ones are best to use for your blog depend largely on your target audience. For example, if you are writing a blog dealing with B2B subjects, you may be better off focusing on LinkedIn. However, if your blog is about celebrity gossip, you may find that Twitter is better for your needs.

Social media is huge and cannot be ignored. However, it needs to be used responsibly otherwise it can end up taking a lot of time with very little return.

How Do I Figure out Which Social Media to Focus on?

This can be a bit tricky, but there are a few ways to go about doing this. First, if you are already active on social media platforms, run Google Analytics and figure out where most of your referral traffic is coming from. If you are getting more attention from Facebook than you are from Twitter, it is probably better to focus more on Facebook.

If you are just getting started, a good way to test the waters is to figure out where your competitors are hanging out. If most of your competition is highly active on LinkedIn, that probably means that your particular vertical is most interesting to people who are on the LinkedIn platform.

You can figure out where your competition is most active by going to their website and plugging it into Alexa.com. You can then look under the "clickstream" tab and see where most of their social media traffic is being driven from. With this information, you can apply it to your own blog.

Another thing to consider is what kind of content you will be generating. If you are going to be working more on long form blog posts, you may do better with Facebook or LinkedIn. If your content is more visual in nature, you may want to try YouTube or Instagram.

Make Sure You Do Not Spread Yourself Too Thin

The trouble with social media is that it is very easy to get sucked into a rabbit hole. There are literally tens of different social media sites that you can focus on, including Facebook, Twitter, LinkedIn, Google Plus, Instagram, Snapchat, StumbleUpon, Quora, Slideshare, Pinterest, Periscope, and several other social media outlets that may cater to more targeted audiences. If you sign up for all of these, there is no way you will be able to maintain an active presence on them all *and* produce a blog. There are not enough hours in the day.

A good strategy for just getting started is to pick two or three of these social media outlets and focus on your presence there. Again, looking at the social media activity of competitors can help you a lot. Not only because you will know what your competitors are doing, but also because you can interact with them on these platforms.

Remember that the nature of social media is that it is social. This means that you cannot operate in a vacuum. While it may seem counterintuitive, actively interacting with your competitors will actually help you generate traffic for your website. If you are sharing things from your competitors, and also commenting on their content, you will also find that this will help you attract the eye of other people who are interested in your subject vertical. We will discuss this more in a later chapter.

But it is very vital to understand that if you are going to be social, you need to actually be social. Not only do you need to interact with your competitors, but you also need to frequently interact with your potential customers. The best brand presences on social media frequently interact with their customers in various ways. For instance, lots of companies that are highly regarded on Instagram will have lots of photo contests. With these contests, they can request user generated photos and then share them.

Not only are these photos excellent marketing material, but they also encourage engagement. The more people that are engaged with your content on social media, the more that they will be engaged with your blog and other outlets. You will need to have a fun, fresh, and most importantly, constant social media presence to really and truly generate quality traffic for your blog.

This is why it is important to not start off with 10 different social media presences. Unless you are paying to outsource your social media, there is no way that you will be able to keep up with all of your social media needs on your own, while also running your blog. It is most important to start off with maybe two or three different presences, and slowly build your way up from there. If your blog does become a success monetarily, you can then outsource your social media and take on additional avenues.

Remember: start small when you start social, and you will start successfully.

Chapter 6: Basic SEO Tips for Traffic Generation

Search engine optimization is a buzzword that has been thrown around the Internet for some time. The reality of the situation is that search engine optimization is necessary if you want to have a successful blog, but the extent that it is necessary is often overestimated. Often, people get a completely incorrect idea of what search engine optimization actually is.

Though, the confusion is not unwarranted. The reason why search engine optimization is so tricky is that nobody actually knows the rules of the game. If you are unfamiliar with search engine optimization, basically it's attempting to up your "page rank" as compared to other websites in your same vertical. Essentially, everybody wants to be on the first page of Google, right? If you are on the first page of Google, your visibility will go up, and more people will engage with and interact with your content.

Attempting to figure out how to optimize your website for maximum search engine ranking is exactly what search engine optimization is. It is a constant balancing act between the proprietors of websites and the search engines. As you might very well be aware, there is a lot of dross on the Internet. People use Google and other search engines to help them filter through all of the bad content to find good content. The reason why Google is such a popular resource is that it is exceptionally good at delivering high-quality content to its users.

Website owners want their websites to be seen as high quality and have search engines like Google display them to searchers who are using particular keywords. So the idea behind effective search engine optimization is to gain a high "page rank" for specific keywords. So, for example, if your blog is about budget travel, you would be keenly interested in appearing on Google's first-page search results for the keyword "budget travel."

However, this is much easier said than done. Google keeps on purposely changing the rules of its algorithm and website owners are constantly trying to figure out these rules. For example, a few years ago website owners discovered that if they simply repeated specific keywords, these would get picked up by the Google algorithm and send their pages to the top of the list.

However, just because content constantly repeats a certain keyword does not necessarily make that content high quality. This led to a practice known as "keyword stuffing" where writers would simply try and jam in desired keywords as many times as possible. Of course, this content was very poor quality and difficult to read. After a while, Google figured this out and it changed its algorithm to punish those who produced keyword-stuffed content.

So, what does this mean for you and your blog? Basically, it's very important to stay on top of current search engine optimization trends and try to apply them to your blog. However, using search engine optimization techniques is akin to using salt in your food. You want to use enough to enhance the flavor of your food, but too much salt will make your food inedible.

Search engine optimization is much like this. You want to use some tactics to try and gain the Google algorithm to your advantage, but you do not want to use too many. Google will actually punish websites that it deems are using search engine optimization to the detriment of content (a concept known as "black hat SEO"). To keep your blog on the good side of Google, you want to use what is known as "white hat SEO" techniques.

If you are looking to get into the world of search engine optimization, we recommend that you start off with these basic tips.

Be specific about the niche of your blog. If you want your blog to naturally benefit from search engine optimization, you need to be specific about what you are actually using that blog to discuss. For example, "travel" is a huge keyword that encompasses many different topics. You will want to focus your search engine optimization attempts on things that are a bit more targeted. For another example, "budget travel" is better and more targeted, but "budget travel in Europe," or "budget travel in Croatia," are much more targeted.

Do not try and spread the focus of your blog too thinly. For example, some people may try and combine "budget travel" with "interior design." This is not a good SEO approach because those two topics have nothing at all to do with each other. It is a better practice to run multiple blogs that focus on different subjects than one blog that tries to focus on many different things.

Understand the power of linking. There are many ways that you can use links to your advantage in the search engine optimization game. Using links correctly will help your standing as an authority source within the Google framework. There are typically two different kinds of links when it comes to external websites. These links are known as "outbound links" and "inbound links."

Outbound links are where you are linking to outside sources of information. If you want to use outbound links to your best benefit, it is best practice linking to other high ranking websites in your vertical. So, for example, if you are writing in the budget travel niche, it may be worthwhile for you to link to websites like Rick Steves or Lonely Planet.

Linking to sources that are seen by Google to be authorities in your vertical will help you seem more legitimate to Google as they prove that you have done your research and you *know* who the powerhouses are in your vertical.

Inbound links. These are when other people link to *your* site. Traditionally these are valued very highly in SEO - if people are linking to your site, it *typically* means that they are considering you an authority source. However, this is complicated; once the black hat SEOs figured out the importance of inbound links, they started out schemes where you could pay to have people link your website on absolutely random other sites. Google discovered this and promptly made the value of inbound links more convoluted.

This is an area that you typically have little control over; unless you are going black hat and paying people to link your site (not recommended), you do not have control over who is linking to your site and when most of the time. *However*, in some instances, you do have control over this, and you should take advantage of it when you do. A good example of this would be putting a guest post on somebody else's blog - if you do this, you should definitely link back to your own site. You can also link to your site by putting it in the signature of your forum or social media presences (if allowed).

The other way that you can play with links is with **internal linking**. That is, if you write a blog post on your blog, link to other blogs you have written or other relevant pages on your site. It's also helpful if you have pertinent lists of links on your main blog page, like your 10 most popular posts.

Your setup does matter slightly with timing and HTML. Some basic HTML tips aren't worth as much as they *used* to be in the SEO game, but they are still worth mentioning.

Use keywords. Picking the right keywords for your website is a challenging game - so much so that some web owners are known to pay thousands of dollars to have somebody pick out great keywords to optimize his or her websites. After all, as mentioned before, your website may be about "travel," but travel is such a broad keyword as to be meaningless. If you want to get that targeted traffic that is specifically looking for what *you* offer, you need to dig down deep and optimize for specific keywords.

There is also an art to the correct way of using keywords. As mentioned earlier, "keyword stuffing" is now a big no-no as far as SEO goes, but this does not mean you should not use *some* keywords in your text. Unlike what many SEO "gurus" will tell you, there actually is no "magic formula" for maximum SEO impact. If your keyword is "budget travel in Croatia," using it two or three times in a 1000-word article will probably be more than enough. You want it to sound natural. A good way to test this is to write your blog post with your keywords and give it to a friend (who isn't familiar with SEO) and ask how it sounds. Ask if they can pick out the keywords. If your friend cannot, then you have done a great job. If the keywords are painfully obvious, they will be to the reader and ultimately to Google.

Use meta tags. Meta tags are a way of embedding keywords into your actual HTML code. If you are using a platform like WordPress or Joomla, there should be a box prompting you for meta tags that does not require you using actual HTML to get them into the script. You do not want to overdo it on the meta tags, but making use of them does provide a small benefit. Simply add your targeted keywords here, and the program will do the rest.

Make use of heading tags. Again, if you are using a blog platform like WordPress, you should see that you get options to use "headers." You should absolutely use these and put your keywords into your headers and subheaders of your text. Not only does using headers and subheaders help break up your blog post into more consumable chunks, but it *also* gives you a boost where Google is concerned. Placing keywords inside your headers and then having them marked by header tags will flag these words as "more important" to Google and give you a bit of an edge.

Be patient. The number one takeaway about search engine optimization is that *it is going to take time*. There is absolutely no way around this fact. If you are doing the "white hat" version of SEO (meaning that you are playing by all the rules and not trying to push funny business past Google), you are going to have to wait a while to see results.

If you are reading between the lines here, you are probably thinking, "all that this chapter said was to write good content and network with others." Those are indeed the key components of SEO. If you want Google to recognize you as somebody that should be highly ranked in your niche, you actually need to *be* highly ranked in your niche by producing high-quality content and also hobnobbing with the important names in your industry.

Again, what many search engine optimization "gurus" seem to miss is that search engine optimization is actually not about trying to cheat the system. The reason why Google re-calibrates its algorithms constantly is to ensure that top quality content gets put front and center. Most "black hat" search engine optimization techniques rarely work for an extended period of time. It's not good enough to merely be on the top of the Google results for two weeks before Google figures out your game and penalizes your site. This is counterproductive.

This is just going to take time. You cannot expect SEO magic to happen overnight. But if you put the necessary amount of time into it and keep on producing great content, your traffic will increase at a slow but steady rate.

Chapter 7: Offer Additional High-Quality Content Outside Your Blog

This may seem counterintuitive; after all, if you want to drive traffic to your blog, shouldn't you be focusing mostly on your blog? The answer to this is both "yes" and "no."

You, of course, want to be working with your blog itself and trying to promote it through various sources (like social media) that we mentioned earlier. However, sometimes you need to think outside the box to get the traffic you crave... or, more precisely, "think outside the blog."

A great way to make your content go further is to repurpose it. We will focus more on reproducing your content to make it either evergreen or to extend the power of a viral post in a later part of this book, but here we would like to discuss the power of eBooks and white papers with you.

While Google is extremely powerful when it comes to traffic generation and should not be ignored, another wonderful way to drive traffic to your blog is by harnessing the power of Amazon. Amazon is a powerful self-publishing platform that has tons of people who are looking for content in your niche. These people are sitting around with credit cards in their hands looking for the exact kind of content that you can offer them.

First of all, exploring what Amazon has to offer will give you an entirely new group of people to work with. Some people do not trust blogs right away and would prefer to purchase a book that is published in their area of interest. Secondly, producing a high-quality book will go very far toward making you seem like an authority in your field, and having the credentials to prove it.

While "publishing" a book may seem like a very daunting and expensive task, thanks to Amazon this could not be further from the truth. It is actually very easy and free to set up an account on Amazon and start publishing books right away. Of course, you will need to ensure that the eBooks you publish are high quality and of use to your readers. You will likely need to do more background research for a quality white paper or eBook as compared to a blog post.

However, if you put the time and effort in, you may be surprised at how far your eBook will reach. Plus, if you have a top ranking eBook on Amazon, this will also affect your Google search results positively. People may search for your topic, and the Amazon result will come up first, with your personal blog beneath it.

To get the most out of an Amazon eBook, there are several tips and tricks that you should take into consideration.

Put an incentive in the eBook itself. Probably the most popular avenue here is to offer consumers a "free report," but this is by far not the only option. You could offer readers of your eBook access to a free course, special interviews, or any other number of additional free goodies to encourage them to visit your blog.

Make sure to link strategically within the eBook. If you are clever enough, you may be able to link to your blog within the part of your eBook that potential buyers can "preview." This means that even if the person does not purchase your eBook, they may click through to your blog anyway.

If you already have a following on your blog, use your eBook as a launch party. If you are lucky enough to already have people interacting with your content on your blog, make sure to harness this if you are publishing an eBook. A great way to get more traffic to your blog is to invite your readers to review your book. Send it to them for review, and if they have a blog, they may post a review there, and link back to *your* blog. This will give you quality inbound links. If they are excited about it, your followers may also advertise your eBook for you through social media.

Take advantage of any traffic that is gained through your eBook. The best way to do this is to create a personalized landing page so that anybody who clicks through to your blog from your ebook gets a personalized greeting. From your landing page, you can also offer a variety of call to actions, including signing up for a newsletter or offering them one of the incentives that you mentioned in your eBook. This will also help you judge how much traffic that your eBook is producing for you.

Depending on what your blog is centered around, eBooks and white papers are not the only options for this. For example, if you are a software developer, offering freeware of various sorts is also a very good way to get traffic to your blog, particularly if your freeware is considered high quality.

Chapter 8: Comment on Other Blogs and Network with Other Bloggers

We mentioned this when we were talking about social media, but networking with other bloggers in your vertical is of extreme importance. One of the biggest mistakes that people make when starting blogs is seeing other blogs in their vertical as competition, rather than potential sources of traffic and thus revenue. To be a successful blog, you need to build and nurture good relationships with other bloggers.

One of the most important things that you can do is figure out whom the authority sources in your vertical are considered to be. For example, if you are looking to start a blog that focuses on content marketing, you definitely need to be paying attention to Content Marketing Institute. If you are looking to get started in food blogging, you definitely cannot ignore The Kitchn.

Once you have ascertained who the authorities are in your particular vertical, you need to become an active commenter on those blogs. It is also advantageous to leave a link to your own blog in your comments, but you want to be careful not to be spamming. If your comments are only about promoting your own blog, it is very likely that they will be filtered out or blocked.

If you comment well enough and if your comments are worthwhile, you will get the attention of these more prominent bloggers. Thoughtful commenting and interaction will help you make positive connections. If you have positive connections with the people in your vertical that are considered the authorities, you stand a high chance of those authorities promoting your content as well. While you should definitely be interacting with the social media outlets of these authority sources, physically commenting on their blogs is likely to get you their attention faster. You can also build a positive reputation with these authority sources through your frequent and thoughtful commenting.

Other than connecting with the actual sources themselves, keep in mind that extremely popular blogs will have many other people who are interested in the vertical interacting in the comments. If you post informative and thoughtful comments, other readers of the authority blog may want to click through to your blog because you seem knowledgeable about the topic as well. This is a great way to generate targeted traffic to your own blog.

Again, this is another way of promoting traffic to your blog that requires quite a bit of effort on your part. There is no way to make a shortcut when it comes to providing thoughtful comments. Sometimes, making informative comments on an authority blog may take more effort than writing your own independent blog post.

However, an advantage to frequently interacting with authority sources is that it will also provide you with a great source of ideas for your own blog. This particularly comes to more topical subjects. If there has been an update to Google, you bet that Content Marketing Institute will be talking about it as will other authority sources. If all of the authority sources are talking about a particular subject, it is an excellent idea for you to address that particular subject on your own blog. Since you have already read the authority sources, you will have a great bank of knowledge to produce a thoughtful blog post of your own.

Working with authority sources and creating relationships with them may even give you the ability to interview them. If you work in the content marketing vertical, and you can get an interview with Ian Laurie, that is going to be extremely powerful, and it is highly likely that it will go viral as he is a huge name in the industry. Again, much of blogging is a "not what you know but whom you know" business.

Few things are more important to successful bloggers than networking. Do not make the mistake of seeing the other blogs in your vertical as competition. Rather, see them as valuable sources of information and assistance that can help you drive valuable traffic to your own blog.

Chapter 9: Email Marketing

Email marketing is a hot button subject for consumers and marketers alike. While there is incredible power in email marketing (almost 20% of marketers say that most of their revenue comes directly from email marketing), it is also an excellent way to annoy your subscribers if it is done incorrectly.

Most people get a deluge of emails every single day. Generally speaking, people will go through their email and sort through the ones that they find valuable or contain information that they must interact with. Thus, if you want people to subscribe to your email marketing list and stay subscribed, you need to offer unique value with your emails.

The definition of "value" is going to be different depending upon the purpose of your blog and also the vertical. Generally speaking, it is more likely that people will sign up for your email marketing list if you offer some kind of monetary incentive. For example, many merchant websites will offer first-time email subscribers a percentage discount off of a purchase if they sign up for the email list.

While this is effective for getting people to sign up for the email marketing list, it's not necessarily effective at getting people to interact with your emails and actually use it to drive traffic. Using email marketing effectively is very difficult, but we have compiled some tips for you.

Have your email come from a person rather than a company. People are much more likely to open emails if it appears to be from an actual person rather than the name of the company. So when your email appears in your customer's inbox, it should say from "John Doe" rather than from "Acme Corporation."

Try to personalize your email as much as possible. Some email marketing platforms will allow you to insert a widget that will address the customer by name when they open your email. This is recommended, as most people are aware that email marketing send outs are not specifically sent to them. Having a little bit of a personalized touch will help encourage people to interact with your email send outs.

Do not make your subject lines too long. Long subject lines are likely to be truncated by email servers. You need to make your email marketing subject lines short and sweet. Not to mention, they also need to be unique and captivating. Something like "Acme Corporation's Email Marketing List" is likely to be deleted. Something like, "You Won't Believe the New Developments at Acme Corporation This Week!" is more likely to grab attention.

Send some snippets of your blog post in your email marketing. Obviously, what you are trying to do here ultimately is drive traffic to your blog, so you definitely should put some teasers from your weekly blog posts in your email marketing. Plenty of people will actually be more likely to read your blog posts if they come to them in email format right at their virtual door as opposed to having to visit your physical blog.

Try to make your email marketing send out a "tips" email. Oftentimes people do not have the time or patience to go through and read an entire blog post. If you want to reach people who are short on time or attention span, try to consolidate your most popular blogs into short "tips" posts. This is almost like turning your blog into a Reader's Digest. This may seem like a tall order, but if you are good at boiling down your blog posts into their most basic elements, you may find that it hooks readers.

Make absolutely sure that your email marketing is optimized for mobile. Did you know that almost half of all emails are opened on mobile devices? It's true. Even worse, only 11% of email marketing templates are actually optimized for mobile. Over half of mobile users will automatically delete email marketing send outs if they are not optimized for mobile, as this makes them difficult to read. You absolutely must make sure that your email marketing send outs can be consumed by mobile users, or you may be inadvertently turning off a great deal of potential traffic.

Do analytics research to send out your email marketing at the right time. It's not just about what you send out, it is also about when you send it. The exact right time for you will depend upon your vertical. For example, if your target audience is business people, you may have best results by sending them out during business hours. If your target audience is stay-at-home moms, you may have better luck sending your emails after 7 PM when the children are in bed. There is no one right answer for all blogs. The best way to do this is to pay attention to when your emails are getting sent out and experiment with different times. Your analytics will tell you when most of your emails are being opened.

If you are simply looking for a baseline to start with, many experts recommend sending out your email marketing lists between 9AM and 12PM. Remember to adjust this based on your time zone. If you are located in the US on the West Coast, you may want to consider sending out your emails earlier than this if most of your traffic is coming from the East Coast.

Additionally, make sure that the "unsubscribe" button is very prominent in your emails. While email marketing can be a popular tool, many people end up with cluttered email boxes, and if somebody really does not want to be a part of your email marketing list, it needs to be easy for them to unsubscribe. Again, email marketing is very powerful, but it can also serve as a point of annoyance.

It is also bad form to end up with people who accidentally subscribed to your email list. Several companies do this by automatically having the "sign me up for the email list" checkbox already checked when doing other things on the website, like making a purchase. Doing this will almost certainly only serve to irritate your readers.

Opting into your email marketing list should be a clear opt, not something that somebody does accidentally.

A reasonably successful way of marketing your email marketing list is to have a brief pop-up that shows up on the screen when somebody visits your blog. Many bloggers do this, and it is quite successful. If you would like to try this, make sure that you put thought into a short but catchy line to encourage people to subscribe, and also consider offering a benefit. Again white papers or discounts on sold items if applicable are good for this.

Make sure that you make email marketing work for you with excellent content and great care for the needs of your readers! Some of your readers will love getting emails from you, while others will consider this more of an intrusion. You want to handle this well to ensure you get best results.

Chapter 10: The Power of Guest Posting

Guest posting is another wonderful way of marketing within your vertical. The nature of guest posting is exactly what it sounds like: you write a post for somebody else's blog. While this may seem counterintuitive, there are many incredible benefits to guest posting. Sometimes, a good guest post can drive hundreds if not even thousands of targeted traffic to your blog.

Again, to take advantage of guest posting, you must have good knowledge of your vertical. For example, if you write in the business vertical, you may know the website business2community.com. This is a very powerful website, and it also allows contributors to guest post on its blog.

Guest posting in this manner will expose you to thousands of new eyes. There are tens of thousands of visitors to business2community each day, who are looking for the kind of content that you are providing if you write in this vertical. Getting the opportunity to guest post on one of these mega-sites can be huge for traffic.

Also, guest posting on another site is a great way for you to get quality inbound links to your blog.

The more quality inbound links you have on other reputable blogs, the more that your website will benefit in the search engine optimization rankings. So once you have found the authority sources in your vertical, make sure you do your research on if they allow guest posting or not.

Sometimes, even if websites do not allow guest posting, if you can build a positive relationship with the owner of the blog they may let you guest post on their website as a favor. This is why networking with other bloggers in your vertical is so very important. You may also be able to do a combined post with them so that you can promote yourself and also show yourself as a close friend of a trusted authority figure.

In addition to guest posting with the more popular authority websites in your vertical, you should also try and network with the smaller fish as well. It is often much easier to arrange guest posting with other bloggers who are not as popular as the bigger websites. You may be able to arrange a guest post exchange with them. That is, you guest post on their website and they guest post on yours. Collaborative efforts like this help to increase your traffic. Even if you guest post on a website that has a smaller audience, that audience may not know you exist, and thus it could translate into targeted traffic gains.

To become successful at guest posting, you also need to be successful at pitching guest posts. First of all, it helps tremendously if the person that you are pitching the guest post to actually knows who you are. The best way to do this is to comment frequently on their blogs and also interact with them on social media. This will make your pitch seem less "cold," and your target will be aware of who you are and that you actually do have valuable insights to bring to the table and also their blog.

If you are looking to increase your chances of having your guest post accepted, it is wise to have written the guest post previous to writing the pitch. The best practice would be to write up the guest post, post it in Google Docs, and then attach a link to the Google Doc in your pitch email.

In the actual pitch itself, make sure that you introduce yourself and state your desire to offer a guest post in your first two sentences. Be clear, polite, and direct. If the person you are pitching to knows you, allude to your previous acquaintance. Additionally, if you have been featured anywhere else or have a unique standing in your vertical, make sure that you mention these as well so that the person reading your email understands the value that you bring to the table.

The Google Doc is helpful because it will allow the other person to read your content and also offer edits if they would like. This turns your guest post into a collaborative effort and ensures that the person whom you are targeting gets ample amount of say in what goes on their blog. Plus, already having a well-written blog posts to offer them shows that you have done your research not only on the subject but also on the readership of your targeted blog. Your chances are much better if you can prove you understand what the readership of the target's blog is looking for.

Once you get permission to make a guest post, it is important that you harness the opportunity and promote it both on your social media outlets and on your own blog. This is particularly important if you manage to get a guest post spot on a high profile authority blog. You may even want to consider paid advertising, as this will help you extend the reach of the blog. Particularly if you are just starting out, paid advertising on guest posts in high authority blogs is usually worth the money.

Guest posting is an outstandingly powerful way to get excellent inbound links and also get your name out there to a wider audience. Again, your success with guest posting will often depend on your success with networking.

Chapter 11: Paid Advertising

You may have noticed that all of the advice we have offered so far to help you generate traffic for your blog has one thing in common: they are free. Of course, many of these avenues will take up a lot of your time (social media is a notorious time stealer), but they do not cost any money. This is one of the beautiful things about the Internet; it is entirely possible to reach a large number of people without having to spend a dime on it.

However, paid advertising certainly does have its place on the Internet, and there is a reason why so many bloggers engage with it. If paid advertising is used well, you can reach a very wide audience of people with very little effort. Sometimes, it's better to spend a few dollars to reach a few thousand people as opposed to spending hours on your twitter account.

However, because paid advertising actually does cost money, it is very important to approach it with a solid plan in mind. You want to make sure that every penny you put toward paid advertising is going to pay off in traffic generation. We have some great tips to help you make that happen.

Make sure you understand your target audience. You should already understand your target audience from writing your blog posts, but what paid advertising helps you do is sidestep all of the dross and go directly after your ideal audience. Not only do you need to know who your ideal customer is, but you also have to understand where they spend most of their time. Does your audience prefer Twitter or Facebook? Is your audience adolescents, stay-at-home parents, business people? Understanding who your target audience is will help you understand how best to reach them.

You need a very succinct call to action. If you are paying for it, you need to know exactly what you want the viewers to do upon seeing your advertisement. Do you simply want them to visit your blog? Do you want them to sign up for your email marketing campaigns? Do you want them to purchase your eBook? Your call to action needed to be strong and pointed for it to reach the customer.

Where can you do advertising for your blog? Probably the two most popular avenues at this point are Google AdWords and Facebook ads.

Facebook ads are incredibly popular and work especially well for those who are trying to target the teen demographic or women. You can experiment with the amount of money you spend on Facebook ads, and the analytics are very helpful.

Meanwhile, Google AdWords work particularly well if you are trying to target a specific demographic based on the location. If you are running something that is locally oriented or if your blog has to do with local subjects, Google AdWords is a very popular avenue for this.

Another thing that you could potentially look into is advertising on specific websites. Not all websites will offer ads, but some authority websites in your vertical may offer space to other resources it deems relevant. In this case, advertising directly on authority sites may prove to be a very keen advantage for you.

Part III:

How to Keep Your Traffic Coming Back

Chapter 12: Repurpose Old Content

One of the most important things you need to learn how to do as a blog owner is to repurpose your old content. Sometimes, even the most creative bloggers can have a hard time coming up with absolutely new material 100% of the time. The good news is that nobody expects you to do this and in fact, it's even counterintuitive. Your readers keep coming back because they like what you have to say. There is no need to reinvent the wheel.

Make sure that you keep a pulse on your content and understand what has performed well and what hasn't. This is why having access to a program like Google Analytics is extremely important. Dig into your analytics and figure out which of your blog posts have performed extremely well and try to figure out why. Do you do best with topical subjects? Or is it your evergreen content that keeps people coming back?

"Evergreen content" is content that will stand the test of time and likely never go out of date. For example, an excellent recipe for your grandmother's chocolate cake is definitely evergreen content. Chocolate cake is not going to become outdated. On the other hand, a post about the very first Google Panda update is definitely topical and will become outdated. Anything regarding the apocalypse back in 2012 is also topical and is now considered outdated.

Content that is evergreen is very easily repurposed, as the information in it is still good. If you have a particular blog post that went viral and is evergreen, there's no reason not to recycle it. In terms of posts that are more topical, you may not be able to recycle the actual content of that blog, but you can take cues from the topic and the angle you took on it to help you create content that is along the same lines.

For example, an excellent way to repurpose "how to" topics in your blog is by taking a series of blog posts and turning them into a guide or eBook. If you had a lot of posts about Twitter advertising that did extremely well, consider taking all of those posts and compiling them into a book. You can then use the book on Amazon or use it as a freebie to entice people to sign up for your email marketing list.

Another excellent way to repurpose evergreen content is to turn it into an infographic. People love infographics; they are very easy and likely to be shared if they are done well. Of course, creating good infographics often requires a considerable amount of artistic skill.

Also, remember that you can repurpose your content to use directly on social media as well. For example, if you have a collection of interesting statistics, those make for fantastic twitter posts. Statistics are short, and often entertaining. Using statistics from a blog post to create a twitter post will help you increase your social media leverage.

Another creative way to recycle good blog post is to consider starting a podcast channel. Many people prefer to listen to their blog post rather than actually read them. In this case, you can literally just read your blog post and not have to rewrite it at all. You may be surprised at the amount of attention you will get if you start a podcast channel. Again, people who sign up for your podcast may be inclined to sign up for your blog.

If you do a lot of work with PowerPoint presentations, those can easily be changed into SlideShare or YouTube posts. If you conduct webinars, those can also be converted into YouTube posts as well.

There are many clever and assorted ways to make use of your old content to keep on using excellent material that shouldn't be left out of the limelight simply because some time has passed! Bringing forward the content that brought your readers to your blog in the first place is an excellent idea to keep your blog fresh, interesting, and timeless.

Chapter 13: Engage with Your Audience

We have spoken extensively about the importance of networking with other bloggers in your vertical. However, if you want to keep your audience coming back for more time and time again, it is important to keep the conversation going with them as well. Remember that in the days of social media and instant communication, readers expect that their blog offers are going to take their concerns and considerations into account. They want to have a "live" experience with you, not have you be an unreachable author on a pedestal.

One of the most important things you can do is be around to answer questions on your blog. Again, this is a good way to make use of your analytics. Study the times of day when your blog gets the most traffic. This is a good time for you to post and then be around to interact with comments in real time if necessary. Anybody who comments on your blog should get a courteous and friendly response. Even if your response is merely "thanks!" this can make a world of difference.

Also, be open to friendly critique or suggestions. Especially if you are running your blog as a one-person operation, it will not be unusual for you to sometimes make typos or other small mistakes. If a commenter on your blog posts out grammatical or factual errors, make sure to thank them for their eagle eyes and then adjust your blog post accordingly with credit. People are more likely to come back to your blog and keep engaging with you if you create an environment of open conversation.

Social media is also extremely important in this. Many people who interact with you on social media will be your readers, not other bloggers. If one of your readers mentioned you in their social media, make sure to take the time to give them a shout out. On some social media platforms, you can even private message people. This is a great way to personally thank individuals for interacting with your content and turn them into loyal readers.

Another way to encourage people to interact with your content is to offer contests or other fun activities. Many high-ranking brands use this to great aplomb, particularly on picture-heavy social media sites like Instagram. If people are participating in your contests with pictures, you can feature those pictures on your main social media platform, the more fun and interactive your brand persona is on social media, the more likely it is that people are going to follow you back and eventually find their way to your blog.

Another wonderful way to interact with your audience is to simply ask them what they want. In your blog, you can occasionally set up polls or other interactive devices to learn more about what your audience specifically wants to read about. People love to be asked their opinions; take advantage of this.

If you are a blogger who proves responsive, informative, and entertaining, people are going to keep coming back again and again. Remember that your content isn't just about the information that you spread, it is also about the person who is providing the content.

Conclusion

Thank for making it through to the end of this book, I hope it was informative and provided you with all of the tools you need to achieve your goals whatever they may be.

The next step is to get out there and get that traffic generated. While it is true that there is no quick fix when it comes to generating the traffic you want for your blog, it also isn't an impossible process. With the right combination of social media and excellent content, you are already well on your way to producing a blog that people in the know will want to read. By doing the research necessary to understand who the authority figures are in your vertical, you can start building credibility by networking with the people who own those blogs.

There are many different avenues to drive traffic to your blog. Paid advertising is certainly a worthwhile avenue when it is used correctly. Networking with other bloggers in your vertical to obtain guest posting privileges will also go leaps and bounds toward gaining the eye of thousands of readers.

Do not forget to use analytics on your posts to understand what your readers love. Understanding how to repurpose that content and gain as much traffic as possible is key to having a successful blog. Email marketing and eBooks can also help you in your quest to promote your blog and gain traffic.

Finally, if you found this book useful in any way, a review on Amazon is always appreciated!

www.ingramcontent.com/pod-product-compliance
Lightning Source LLC
Chambersburg PA
CBHW031622210526
45464CB00004B/1700